me and my sewing machine

me and my sewing machine

a beginner's guide

Kate Haxell

stash

fabric arts for a handmade lifestyle

First published in the
United States in 2010 by
C&T Publishing, Inc.
PO Box 1456,
Lafayette, CA 94549

www.ctpub.com

Photography Dominic Harris
Design Louise Leffler

This book was conceived and
produced by Breslich & Foss Ltd
Unit 2a Union Court
20-22 Union Road
London SW4 6JP

Library of Congress
Cataloging-in-Publication
data available upon request.

ISBN 978-1-60705-078-0

Printed and bound in China

10 9 8 7 6 5 4 3 2 1

3 9082 11748 4728

CONTENTS

6 Introduction

8 My sewing machine
18 Getting ready to sew
28 Seams simple
40 Hemmed in
50 Fastened up
64 Around the corner
72 On the edge
84 Fancy that
96 Make me, make me!

126 Glossary
127 Template
127 Resources
128 Index

Introduction

Turning a piece of flat fabric into a three-dimensional item that is both useful and beautiful is the most extraordinarily satisfying pastime. You have bought this book (or some lovely person has given it to you) because you, too, want that satisfaction, and so I'm delighted to welcome you to the truly global sewing circle.

I don't remember my first stitches, though I do remember sitting cross-legged in primary school sewing something or another: the unfortunate Julia Lloyd stitched right through her project and sewed it to her skirt. I earned pocket money sewing name labels into all of my three brothers' school clothes, even their socks. I was paid (with hindsight, rather poorly) by the label and both my mother (who didn't love sewing) and I were happy.

My skills have progressed since then, learned piecemeal from better sewers, from magazines, from getting it wrong the first time, and from books. However, I've always found the vast sewing tomes rather off-putting. There's just such a huge amount of information: am I expected to know it all? What on earth for? So this is a different kind of sewing book. From what to look for when buying your sewing machine, through the practicalities of seams, hems, and fastenings, to the decorative delights of ruffles, pleats, and ribbons, this book contains information and techniques you need to know to sew well using your sewing machine—and nothing more.

There are no scary couture-type techniques that real sewers never use, no painstaking procedures that don't actually make your sewing easier, or help it look better, and no complicated methods of doing anything. Instead you will find step-by-step methods that make sewing simple, even if you have never used a machine before.

I hope that you and your sewing machine become the best of friends and that you revel in the world it opens up for you.

Kate Haxell

My sewing machine

A sewing machine doesn't have to be an expensive purchase these days: you can buy a basic, inexpensive new machine or hunt on internet auction sites for a bargain. If you decide to do the latter, do take as much care as possible to ensure that what you are buying is all it seems to be.

How a sewing machine works

Nearly all modern sewing machines work in basically the same way. There will be variations in the way the bobbin goes in, the way you thread the top spool, and the way you select functions, but the underlying principles will be similar.

You certainly don't need a detailed technical explanation of how all machines do everything, but some information is useful—so here are some photographs of my sewing machine with captions telling you what is what.

In the manual that comes with your sewing machine there should be photographs like these ones, or diagrams, that tell you about that particular machine. If you don't have a manual, contact the machine's manufacturer and see if they can send you one, or check on the internet to see if there is one you can download. Alternatively, if you have a friendly local sewing store, take your machine in and ask them to explain it to you.

Side view

handwheel: turn this to manually raise or lower the needle

power switch

power socket: where the foot pedal— which makes the machine run—is plugged in

Front view

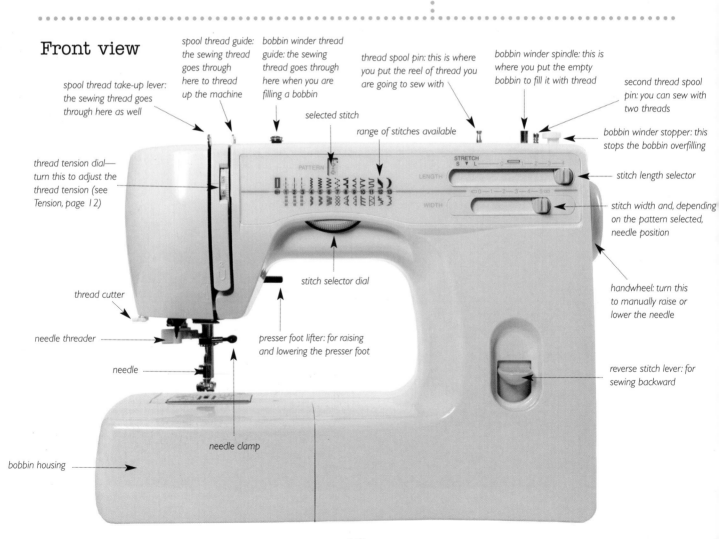

spool thread take-up lever: the sewing thread goes through here as well

spool thread guide: the sewing thread goes through here to thread up the machine

bobbin winder thread guide: the sewing thread goes through here when you are filling a bobbin

thread spool pin: this is where you put the reel of thread you are going to sew with

bobbin winder spindle: this is where you put the empty bobbin to fill it with thread

second thread spool pin: you can sew with two threads

selected stitch

range of stitches available

bobbin winder stopper: this stops the bobbin overfilling

thread tension dial— turn this to adjust the thread tension (see Tension, page 12)

stitch length selector

stitch width and, depending on the pattern selected, needle position

stitch selector dial

handwheel: turn this to manually raise or lower the needle

thread cutter

needle threader

presser foot lifter: for raising and lowering the presser foot

reverse stitch lever: for sewing backward

needle

needle clamp

bobbin housing

Needle, presser foot, and throat plate

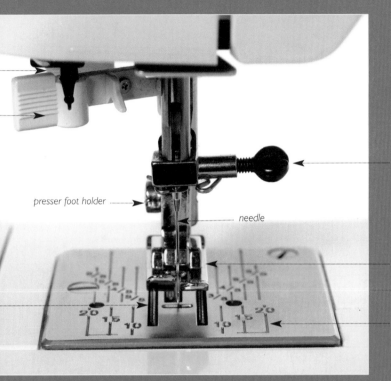

one-step buttonhole lever

needle threader: a useful optional feature if you struggle to thread fine needles

presser foot holder

needle

feed dogs: these feed the fabric under the needle at a rate controlled by how hard you press the power pedal

needle clamp: this holds the needle in the machine

presser foot: this is lowered to sit on top of the fabric. There are different feet for different sewing tasks

throat plate with measurements marked

Hook race and bobbin case

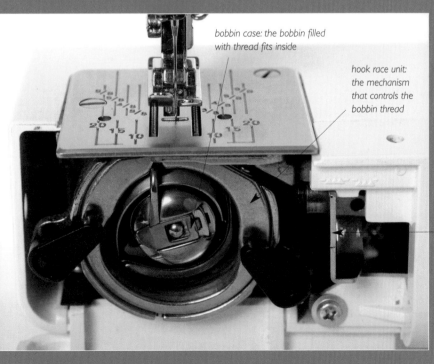

bobbin case: the bobbin filled with thread fits inside

hook race unit: the mechanism that controls the bobbin thread

feed dog drop lever: for dropping the feed dogs to do free-motion embroidery

Tension

All sewers, novices and skilled seamstresses alike, sometimes wonder if the machine's tension is what is causing their tension. Incorrect thread tension is probably the most common sewing problem and it can completely ruin a project.

The first thing to understand is what sewing machine tension actually is. The term "tension" refers to the amount of pressure on the sewing thread coming from the top reel. This pressure is exerted by the tension discs, which are inside the machine and through which the sewing thread passes when you thread up the machine.

Different fabrics and stitches need different amounts of tension. The tension is controlled by the thread tension dial on the front of the machine (see page 10). Turning the dial to a higher number increases the tension and to a lower number, decreases it. On most machines,

turning the dial to number 5 will give you a tension suitable for straight stitch on mediumweight fabric.

If the bobbin thread is visible on the right side of the fabric or the spool thread is visible on the wrong side, then the tension is not set correctly. Also, if seams are puckered, the thread keeps breaking, knotting, or jamming the machine, or stitches are getting skipped, then incorrect tension could be the cause.

Before you start a project, always test the tension on a scrap of the project fabric. Fold it double to check how seams will sew; if you are using lining or interfacing, add a scrap of that; test the stitches you are planning to use. Duplicate all aspects of the project in miniature and get the tension right—this really is worth the time and effort. If you skip this testing then any tension problems can spoil your project.

Balanced tension

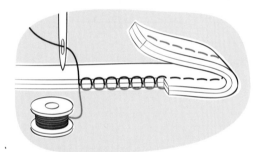

If the tension is set properly, then the bobbin and spool threads interlock within the layers of fabric, as above. Only the spool thread is visible on the right side and only the bobbin thread on the wrong side.

Top tension too loose

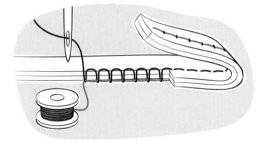

If the spool thread is visible on the wrong side, then the top tension is too loose. Try sewing a line of stitching with a reel of contrast thread on the spool pin. Dots of the contrast color on the wrong side will tell you that the top tension needs increasing. Turn the dial to a half number higher and sew a test, as before.

Top tension too tight

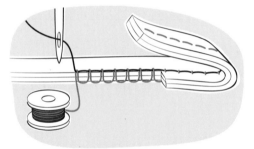

If the bobbin thread is visible on the right side, then the top tension is too tight. If you are unsure as to whether this is the problem, put a contrast color thread on the bobbin and sew a line of stitching on a scrap of the project fabric. If you can see dots of the contrast color on the fabric, then the top tension is indeed too tight. Turn the thread tension dial to a half number lower and sew another line. Continue decreasing the tension by half a number until it is balanced.

A tension test

Sew a line diagonally across a square of fabric, so that the stitching is on the bias (see Making Bias Strip and Binding, pages 74–75). Hold the ends of the stitched line firmly and pull hard so the fabric stretches. If only the top thread breaks, then the top tension is too tight. If only the bottom thread breaks, then the top tension is too loose. If both threads break, then the tension is balanced.

More tension issues

If you've adjusted the tension dial but are still having problems, then check the following as they may be affecting tension.

Have you threaded the machine correctly, top and bottom? Pull the top thread out and thread it up again. If the machine is new, check the manual to make sure you're not missing out a stage. Take out the bobbin and re-insert it, again checking that you are doing it properly.

How long have you been using the needle? If you've been sewing with the same needle for some time then it might be blunt or bent. Just pulling on the fabric can bend a needle and the tiniest defect can cause problems. Change the needle, making sure you select the right one for the fabric (see pages 22–23). In fact, you should change the needle regularly: "new project, new needle" is a good motto.

Is the machine clean? As you sew, lint from the fabrics builds up in the machine. If you don't clean it regularly then the hook race and bobbin case (see page 11) can get clogged with lint and this will cause sewing chaos. A little brush for cleaning out these components should have come with the machine, so use it.

What kind of thread are you using? If you are sewing with a cheap thread you picked up in a market, then try swapping it for a good-quality, brand-name thread (see Threads, page 23).

Are you using a plastic bobbin? If you are, is it elderly? Nicks in the rim of a bobbin, even tiny ones, can catch the thread. Swap the bobbin for a new one and see if that cures the problem.

The other tension

The bobbin case also has a tension adjustment, but you should only use it if you really can't fix the problem by adjusting the top tension, and you have checked that thread, needle, or lint issues aren't the cause of the trouble.

Usually, you would only expect to adjust the bobbin case tension if you were using a thick or decorative thread on the bobbin. Machine embroiderers, who often do use fancy bobbin threads, may have two bobbin cases; one that is never adjusted and is used for regular sewing, and one for their fancy threads, which is fiddled with at will.

To alter the bobbin case tension, you use a special screwdriver (which should be supplied with your machine) to turn the tiny screw in the bobbin case. Turn it to the left to decrease the tension and to the right to increase the tension. Hold the bobbin case over an empty box while you do this, because if the tiny screw falls out it's very difficult to find again.

Make a note of the direction you turned the screw in and how far you turned it so that you can re-set the tension to the factory setting when or if you need to.

Buying your first sewing machine

The first step in buying your own sewing machine is to decide which functions you are going to need. Modern sewing machines range from very basic models that do little more than sew straight lines, to computerized machines with a myriad of features to make your head spin. You are almost certainly going to want something in between.

For a first sewing machine you need a model that is simple enough to use easily and yet sophisticated enough to grow into. You won't want to spend too much on your first machine, just in case you decide sewing's not the craft for you, but bear in mind that a really cheap machine may not sew very well.

I recommend choosing a mid-range machine from a good brand name. This way you get a decent machine and you'll be able to buy extra accessories: the big brands produce wide ranges of these. Most manufacturers are sensible and accessories produced for one machine will fit their other models. So when you upgrade your machine, stay with the same brand and you don't have to buy everything again.

Sewing machines of this type will have the basic straight and zigzag stitches plus some extras, which are all you'll need. One function I do recommend you look for is an automatic, one-step buttonhole. Doing buttonholes manually on the sewing machine is perfectly possible, but doing them automatically is less stressful, quicker, and usually better-looking (see pages 58–59).

Another useful feature is a variable needle position; this makes it easier to sew straight lines in odd places as you can align the fabric with a throat plate guide or the edge of the presser foot and then move the needle across to sew in the required spot.

If possible, borrow a machine for a few days and have a good play with it. Check out all the functions and see what you think will be most useful. If you are lucky enough to have a local store that is not dedicated to one brand of sewing machine, then it's certainly worth asking the staff for recommendations. Otherwise, spend some time browsing the internet and compare reviews.

Sewing machine accessories

Your sewing machine will come with some accessories and to start with you won't need to buy more. As you develop your skills and master new techniques, you'll find some of the items shown useful, though you should buy them as and when you need them. Depending on the make of sewing machine you buy, its presser feet may not look exactly like the ones shown, but they'll do the same things.

Straight foot
This foot is for sewing simple straight lines (see Sewing Straight Lines, page 30), and so is the one you'll use most of the time.

Zigzag foot
The foot you'll use for zigzag stitch and for some automatic decorative stitches (see Stitches, page 23).

Zipper foot
These vary a lot in style, but they are all designed to let you stitch as close to the zipper teeth as possible (see pages 52–57 for different types of zippers).

Patchwork foot
The right-hand side toe of this foot is ¼" (5mm) wide, so it's useful as a guide for narrow seams. I don't do much patchwork (see Patchwork, page 94), but I use this foot quite a lot.

Clear view foot
This is useful for appliqué because you can easily see what you are doing (see Appliqué, page 93). This one has a recess underneath that allows it to pass smoothly over a line of satin stitch.

Teflon foot
A super-smooth foot that glides over "sticky" fabrics, such as vinyl.

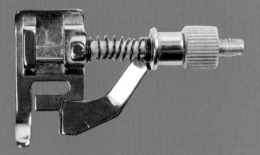

Blind hem foot
The adjustable right-hand toe lets you set the hem to the required depth (see Blind-stitch Hem, page 44).

Free-motion embroidery foot

This is another foot that varies a lot in style. The open-toe versions, like this one, let you easily see what you are doing (see Free-motion Embroidery, page 92).

Walking foot

This foot helps to feed layers of fabric evenly through the machine when quilting (see Quilting, page 95). They are usually expensive and not always necessary for simple quilting projects.

Automatic buttonhole foot

You fit the button in place and the buttonhole is sewn to the correct size to fit it (see Automatic Buttonhole, page 58).

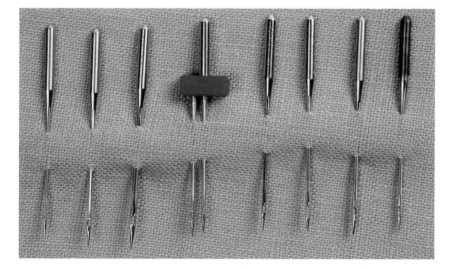

Sewing machine needles

Picking the right needle for the fabric you are using will make a real difference to your sewing. Shown here, left to right: 60/8, 80/12, 110/18, twin needle, 75/11 embroidery needle, 80/12 metallic thread needle, 90/14 leather needle, 80/12 ballpoint needle.

For advice on which needle to use with which fabric, turn to Fabrics, Threads, and Stitches, pages 22-23.

Quilting guide

This fits onto the presser foot to help you sew evenly spaced lines (see Quilting, page 95).

Magnetic guide

This clamps onto the throat plate to help you sew straight lines (see Sewing Straight Lines, page 30).

Sewing tools and equipment

As well as the basics—such as scissors—here are numerous tools and gadgets you can buy to help you with your sewing. These are items I have bought and actually use, as opposed to pieces that live undisturbed in the box they came in.

I have five different pairs of scissors in my workbox, of which you'll need three: fabric shears, embroidery scissors, and paper scissors. In addition I have pinking shears and thread snips. I don't buy expensive scissors, but I do take care of them and never use my fabric scissors for cutting paper—it's a sure way to dull the edges of the blades.

Fabric shears
There are different styles available, but ones like these with a bent handle make cutting out fabric easy.

Embroidery scissors
Look for ones with very sharp points and short, slim blades.

Thread snips
I find these very useful for quickly and easily trimming thread ends while machining.

Seam ripper
This is designed for cutting out seams that have gone wrong. Slip the long toe under the stitches and gently push to cut through the thread.

Thimble
This is used for pushing a hand-sewing needle through thick fabric. I prefer rubber thimbles to metal ones.

Pins
I use very long, fine pins with glass heads that can be ironed over without melting. The length and slimness means that they don't mark fabrics and make minimal ripples. I always use magnetic pincushions (this one was designed to be a paperclip holder). Although they do magnetize the pins, they are very convenient.

Hand-sewing needle
You'll sometimes need one of these for finishing off bits of projects. The larger the size number, the finer the needle is.

Whatever measuring system you use—metric or imperial—stick to it and don't chop and change between the two or you'll end up in a measuring mess. This book has both styles of measurement for every technique and project.

Seam gauge

I use this all the time for measuring short distances, such as for hems and seams. Set the red slider to the required distance and it's quick and easy to measure and check.

Cloth tape measure

This is indispensable; wear it draped around your neck to feel like a true seamstress.

Long and short rules

These are useful, but not essential, though mine do have a permanent home in my workbox.

There are various fabric markers available. The two types I use are a water-soluble marker and tailor's chalk. Air-soluble markers are good, but I find that too often the mark has disappeared before I've finished the project. Whichever marker you use, always test it on a scrap of the fabric first to ensure it will completely disappear.

Bias binding maker

A great bit of kit for making your own bias binding.

Bobbin ring

A neat piece of equipment for storing bobbins, items that otherwise end up in a tangled mess in your workbox.

Water-soluble fabric marker

Remember that water can mark fabrics, so when you test the marker on the fabric, wet it and iron it dry to check that no watermarks appear.

Tailor's chalk

The classic fabric marker, the chalk easily brushes off most fabrics.

Getting ready to sew

There are a few basic bits of knowledge and some general skills that you'll find useful for whichever techniques in this book you are going to tackle. Read this chapter through before you launch into any sewing—it's worth it.

A space for sewing

The vast majority of home sewers don't have the luxury of a dedicated sewing room and instead have to make do with space stolen from the guest bedroom or a corner of the living room. However, a small space can be perfectly effective if you organize it well.

You are going to need a sturdy table, a comfortable, straight-back chair, and an iron and ironing board close by. If you have the iron in another room you may not want to get up and go to press the fabric when you should and your sewing will suffer as a result (see Pressing, pages 26–27). In an ideal world the table will be big enough to cut out fabric on as well as hold the sewing machine. If this isn't possible, then you can cut out on the floor—make sure it's clean first.

Sewers, like knitters, quite quickly build up a stash. Delicious fabrics, gorgeous trims, colorful threads, and cute buttons are irresistible, and can take up a surprisingly large amount of space. If you don't organize them properly then you'll never be able to find the prefect piece when you need it. You'll go out and buy another and your stash will just grow and grow, full of many similar things.

I like to use see-through storage as much as possible: I keep small pieces of fabric folded in clear plastic, stackable crates and I store buttons by color in plastic button tubes. Larger pieces of fabric are folded in a cupboard, organized by fiber. Ribbons and trims are wound and clipped with mini wooden clothes pegs (originally sold as office stationery, though I don't know what you are supposed to do with them in that context).

An excellent way to store sewing spools of thread is on a DIY rack (see below left): mine is mounted on the outside of a cupboard door as I think the threads are so decorative. To make a spool rack, you hammer nails into strips of wooden molding then screw the molding to the door. Slip the cotton reels onto the nails, arranging them by color for best effect. If you're more of a shopper than a DIYer, then you can buy ready-made wooden spool racks.

A capacious workbox—but not too big to carry—to hold all your sewing machine accessories and other bits of sewing kit is a must. I use a mechanic's toolbox as it has fold-out trays and lots of space, but there are many dedicated sewing boxes available.

It doesn't really matter how you organize and store your stash and equipment as long as you know where things are and can get to them easily. Inefficient storage is almost as bad as no storage at all.

Office pedestals

The wheeled pedestals sold for office use can make excellent sewing storage. There's usually a big drawer in the bottom for hanging files—fabrics can go in there. The smaller drawers hold trims, threads, and kit, and the very slim top drawer with the partitions for pens and paperclips is great for presser feet, pins, and other little items. As the whole thing is on wheels, it can easily be brought out and stashed away as needed.

How to run a sewing machine

Once you have got your new sewing machine home, the very first thing to do is to read the manual. Even if you have used a sewing machine before, different makes and models have different operating details and, if you don't read the instructions, you can end up damaging your machine before you've finished your first sewing project.

Set up the machine on a sturdy table. A decorator's folding table, or even a gate-leg table, are not good choices because when a machine is running at full pelt it can bounce to an alarming degree if the table isn't solid, and that really will ruin your sewing. Pull up a straight-back, armless chair—a dining chair is good, but not a wheeled office chair as they move too easily—and check that the machine is at the right height for you to operate it comfortably. Can you reach the power pedal easily without stretching your leg? Is the power cable safely out of the way and not stretched tightly to the machine so that if you trip over it you'll pull the machine off the table? Is the machine high enough for you to see the fabric going under the needle without craning your neck? But low enough for you to sew without having to lift your arms uncomfortably high? All ok? Excellent!

With the manual read, the machine set up, a medium straight stitch selected and a piece of fabric to experiment with chosen, you are ready to start sewing. The first thing to do is to sew a line, check the stitch tension, and adjust it if necessary (see Tension, page 12).

Then you need to get your hands in the right position. Novice sewers sometimes hold the fabric as shown on above right, with one hand clutching the front edge and the other at the back pulling the fabric through. This is not how to sew. The feed dogs (see page 11) feed the fabric through the machine at a rate controlled by how hard you press the power pedal; you don't need to help them do their job.

Pulling the fabric like this is also an easy way to bend the needle. They are only slivers of metal and they bend easily, and then you can have all sorts of tension problems (see Tension, page 12).

Your job is to guide the fabric so that it passes under the needle where you want the stitching to be. To this end, have both hands resting lightly on the fabric, fairly flat and quite close to the presser foot, as shown on below right. Obviously you want to avoid sewing your fingers, but that is reasonably easy to do. NEVER take your eyes off the needle when it's moving. If someone calls you, stop sewing, then look up. Don't sew in front of the television where you'll be tempted to glance at the action on screen.

Position the fabric under the presser foot with the edge against one of the marks on the throat plate (see Sewing Straight Lines, page 30). Get comfortable in your chair and put your hands on the fabric. GENTLY press the power pedal. As the fabric runs under the needle and away from you, keep moving your hands so that they stay in the same position in relation to the needle, and gently steer the fabric so that the edge of it stays against the same mark on the throat plate.

Get used to how the fabric moves under the needle, then press the pedal a little harder. Sew back and forth across the piece of fabric, changing speeds and stitch patterns until you are comfortable sewing: this may take more than one session. However, it's well worth continuing to experiment and practice on non-lovely fabric until you are really confident with your machine before starting a project. If you are still at the practice stage, any project will suffer and you'll be discouraged and that's never good.

The wrong way to hold the fabric when sewing.

The right way to steer the fabric when sewing.

Fabrics, threads, and stitches

There is an absolutely huge range of fabrics available to today's sewer, far too huge a range to discuss in detail here. On these pages there is an overview of the most popular sewing fabrics, plus a little advice on threads and stitches.

Fabrics

There'll usually be two main reasons why you choose a fabric for a project; one is practical—how suitable the fabric is—and one is aesthetic—how much you like the fabric. Try not to choose a fabric solely for the second reason, as it could mean that your project just doesn't work out no matter how carefully you sew.

Left, from the top the fabrics in this pile are:

Lace Most modern lace fabrics are made from man-made fibers, though you can buy gorgeous, and expensive, silk and cotton lace. Lace is mainly used for bridal and evening gowns, overlaid on another fabric. It isn't especially difficult to sew, though very delicate and vintage lace can be fragile. Use a fine needle from an 8/60 to an 11/75.

Lining fabric Generally made from synthetic fibers, lining materials come in a myriad of solid colors and great patterns. I love using fancy lining; even if no one else sees it, you know it is there and it makes a garment that bit more special. Linings are slippery and can be really tricky to sew, so I recommend basting (see Basting, page 25). For real luxury, you can buy silk lining fabric that feels wonderful next to your skin. Sew synthetic lining with an 11/75 or a 12/80 needle and silk lining with an 11/75 or finer.

Tweed This is a traditional Irish wool tweed and is thick and heavy—ideal for a warm winter coat. It's easy enough to sew, though as it's such a chunky weave it does fray quite easily. Sew it with a 14/90 or 16/100 needle.

Silk This is dupioni silk, which is probably the easiest silk fabric to sew as it's the least slippery. However, it frays madly, marks easily, and will shift around given the chance. Having said that, silk looks and feels so lovely that it's hard to resist for a special dress. Baste your seams (see Basting, page 25), finish all raw edges (see Finishing Edges, page 32), and be very careful of watermarks when pressing (see Pressing, pages 26–27). Sew silk with an 11/75 needle or finer.

Suedette A fake suede fabric made from synthetic fibers, this comes in a limited range of colors. It's not the easiest fabric to sew because, like velvet, when two layers are right sides facing they try to "creep" along one another and create an uneven seam. Firm, short-stitch basting (see Basting, page 25) will help keep this fabric under control. Lightweight suedette can be sewn with a 12/80 or 14/90 needle. For heavier suedettes (and real suede) use a 14/90 or 16/100 leather needle.

Wool Versatile, available in different weights, colors, and patterns, and easy to sew, wool is a wonderful fabric. Be careful pressing it (see Pressing, pages 26–27), as too much heat and steam can felt the surface. Sew lightweight wools with a 12/80 needle, moving up to a 16/100 for the heaviest weights.

Printed cotton The most popular sewing fabric in the world. You can buy cotton fabric in almost any color and design you could want, and it has many different names. Do check the fiber content on "cotton" fabrics as they can have a man-made fiber mixed in, which you may or may not want. Remember that with large-scale patterns you may want to pattern-match at the seams, so you'll need to buy extra fabric and baste the seams (see Basting, page 25). Generally easy to sew, choose an 11/75 needle for the lightest weight cottons—such as chambray—going up to a 18/110 for thick cotton duck. Mediumweight dressmaking cotton can be sewn with a 12/80.

Satin Often made from synthetic fibers, satin can be lovely to look at and really horrid to sew. It slips, shifts around, marks at the first possible opportunity, and often doesn't press well. If you're absolutely set on using satin, baste (see Basting, page 25) everything within the seam allowances and sew with an 11/75 needle.

Velvet This is velvet with a crushed finish, which does make this a slightly more forgiving fabric than straight-pile velvet. However, velvet is for experienced sewers only: it's probably the most difficult fabric there is to sew beautifully. You need to baste (see Basting, page 25) every seam using irregular long and short stitches, ideally sew it with a walking foot (see Sewing Machine Accessories, page 14), and press it on a special needleboard with paper under the seam allowances to stop them making an impression on the right side. And it frays like nothing else on earth. If you really, really must have velvet, then sew it with great care and a 12/80 or 14/90 needle.

Solid-color cotton All the attributes of printed cotton with none of the pattern-matching issues. Perfect!

Corduroy Usually made from cotton—sometimes with synthetic fiber mixed in—corduroy is hardwearing and fairly easy to sew. In a similar way to velvet, the furry finish can "creep" a little when you are sewing two pieces right sides together, so basting (see Basting, page 25) is a good idea. Use a 14/90 needle to sew corduroy.

Threads

The golden rule for threads is not to buy cheap ones. They'll usually be poor quality, will snap, fray, and there won't be very much on the spool so you'll run out quickly.

To avoid potential laundering complications, sew fabrics with thread made of the same fiber whenever you can. So, use cotton thread for cottons, silk thread for silks, and polyester thread for man-made fibers and for woolen fabrics, as there is no such thing as wool thread.

Rayon and metallic threads are generally used for machine embroidery (see Free-motion Embroidery, page 92) and should be sewn with a metallic or embroidery needle, which have a very sharp point and an elongated eye to help them pierce the fabric smoothly and easily.

Stitches

Basic manual machines might offer fewer than ten different stitches, while the computerized sewing machines can produce dozens of fancy stitches, so we can't look at everything here. However, most of the time you'll only use a few stitches and we can look at those.

Below, from the left these stitches are:
Straight stitch There are three different stitch lengths shown here. A very short stitch, a medium stitch—the one you'll usually use—and a long stitch that's used for gathering and machine basting.

Stretch straight stitch This is a more elastic version of straight stitch and should be used to sew stretchy woven and knit fabrics.

Zigzag stitch Used to finish edges (see Finishing Edges, page 32), this stitch can be set to different widths and tightness.

Satin stitch This is a wide, tight zigzag stitch used for edging appliqué motifs (see Appliqué, page 93).

Tricot stitch This is the version of zigzag stitch that you use to finish the edges (see Finishing Edges, page 32) of stretchy fabrics.

Overcast stitch Another stitch that's used to finish edges (see Finishing Edges, page 32).

Box stitch Used to join pieces of batting for quilting (see Quilting, page 95). Overlap the edges of the batting by ⅜" (1cm) and sew a line of box stitch along the overlap for a smooth, non-bulky join.

Embroidery stitches The last two stitches are automatic embroidery stitches. These can offer a quick and easy way of adding detail to a project.

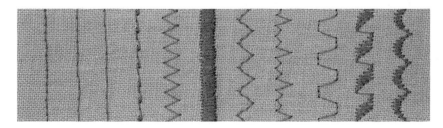

Pinning

Putting pins in pieces of fabric to hold them together may not sound like it needs any instructions, but there are a couple of tricks that'll make your machine sewing easier and help prevent you pricking yourself more often than absolutely necessary.

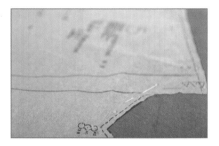

Pinning for machine sewing

Pin like this and you'll never have the annoyance of the head of the pin facing the needle as you sew toward it, making it difficult to take out.

Match the edges of the fabrics to be joined and have the raw edge facing away from you. If it's a hem, fold the edge up and have the fold facing away from you. Starting at the point where you'll start sewing, put in pins with the heads facing to the right. As you sew the seam the heads will all face you, ready to be easily pulled out before the needle reaches them.

Pinning for basting

If you're pinning prior to basting, then do it like this to avoid pricking yourself as you sew.

Match the edges of the fabrics to be joined and have the raw edge facing toward you. If it's a hem, fold the edge up and have the fold facing toward you. Starting at the point you'll start basting, put the pins in with the heads facing to the right. As you baste toward them the heads, not the points, of the pins will be facing you.

Pinning pattern pieces

Pinning paper patterns to fabric needs to be done carefully and well to make sure that the piece of fabric you cut out is in fact the same shape as the paper pattern piece.

Firstly, make sure the fabric is smooth and flat. If it has wrinkles or folds, press them out (see Pressing, pages 26–27). Lay the pattern piece on the fabric and smooth it flat with your hands: if it's very wrinkled, then iron it with a warm, dry iron. Put in lots of pins, making sure that all points and valleys are held to the fabric. The full length of each pin must be within the pattern piece so that you don't nick the blades of your fabric scissors when you cut around the paper.

Sewing over pins

My grandma, who taught me to sew, didn't hold with this and I never do it, but other sewers I know do. I include the technique here, but if you're going to use it, do so with caution.

Match the edges of the fabrics to be joined and put the pins in at right angles to the raw edge, leaving the heads protruding. Sew the seam fairly slowly, sewing over the shafts of the pins. Take the pins out once the stitching is complete.

The reasons I don't hold with sewing over pins are firstly that you quite often hit a pin with the needle, at best making an irregular stitch and at worst breaking the needle. Pins can wrinkle the fabric if they're not placed properly, and then you sew the wrinkle into the seam. Finally, if the fabrics need holding together while you sew then it really doesn't take long to baste them.

Cutting out

Accurate cutting is essential for accurate sewing. The aim is to cut the fabric while keeping it as flat as possible on the work surface: lifting the fabric almost guarantees wobbly cut edges.

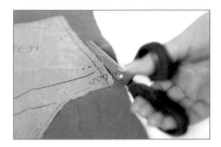

Fabric scissors with bent handles allow the blades to cut close to and parallel to the work surface, lifting the fabric only a little, without your having to contort your hand into an odd position.

Open the blades as wide as is comfortable for your hand and slip the lower blade under the fabric where you want to start cutting. Close the blades smoothly, cutting the fabric, but do not close them fully. Just before the tips of the blades close, open them wide again and slide the lower blade further under the fabric along the cutting line. Cutting this way (without fully closing the blades) will help avoid snags and dips in the cut edge.

Basting

In today's hurry-along world, anything that takes a little more time is often cast aside whether or not it's useful, and basting can be so very useful. I'm not saying you should *always* baste, but for slippery fabrics, shaped seams, trims, and neat zippers, pinning and hoping won't usually be enough.

Seams and hems

For seams or hems in fabrics that aren't inherently tricky to sew (see Fabrics, page 22), you only need to baste if the seam is shaped or the hem is curved.

Pin the fabric along the basting line (see Pinning for Basting, opposite). Thread a slim needle with thread the length of the line to be basted plus 6" (15cm). If this is ridiculously long and impossible to use, then you'll need to baste the line in two sections.

Sew a line of running stitch, with stitches about ⅜" (1cm) long, along the basting line.

The basting line doesn't need to be measured and marked, as it doesn't matter if it is a bit wobbly. The stitches don't have to be neat and even, though they should be firm and not too long or they won't do their job.

Slippery fabrics and fabrics with pile—such as velvet—should always be basted and it's best to use the long-and-short technique. This involves making firm stitches that vary in length between ¼" (5mm) and ⅜" (1cm): the irregularity in stitch length helps to keep the layers of fabric from shifting.

Taking the needle in and out of the fabric to put several stitches on it before pulling the thread through, as shown here, is a quick and perfectly valid way of basting a seam or hem. However, when putting in a zipper or basting a tricky corner, you may well find it better to make individual stitches.

Where to baste

One of the most common mistakes novice sewers make is to baste precisely where the line of machine sewing will be. They then have to spend time picking out the basting stitches without damaging the machine stitches.

So, whenever possible, baste a little distance from where you will machine sew. For a seam with a standard ⅝" (1.5cm) seam allowance, baste about ⅜" (1cm) from the edge of the fabric. If you are machining a hem and will have the edge of the presser foot against the fold, then baste right next to the fold.

Pressing

When you're making a sewing project, you should be using your iron almost as much as your sewing machine. Proper, accurate pressing will make the most enormous difference to your sewing, on both a practical and an aesthetic level.

The practicalities of pressing

There is a difference between pressing and ironing. Ironing involves moving the iron around on the fabric and is what you do to freshly laundered garments. Pressing involves placing the iron in one spot, then lifting it and placing it in another, without dragging on the fabric.

If at all possible, set up your iron and ironing board in the room you sew in (see A Space For Sewing, page 20). You should press your project every time you sew a section of it, and if the iron is to hand and you don't have to leave the room, then you are more likely to be good about doing this.

Check what temperature your fabric can be pressed at. Generally, cotton and linen can be pressed with a hot iron, wool with a warm iron and synthetics with a cool iron. However, this isn't a firm rule and introducing steam can change things, so you need to test a scrap of fabric first to check that you have the right temperature.

Before using steam on a fabric, check that any watermarks you might make on the fabric will disappear. Drop a little water on to a scrap of the fabric and iron it dry, then check that no watermark remains. Steam has two functions: it helps take out very stubborn folds and creases and it will "set" fabric into a shape. How firm the "set" will be depends on the fabric, and it will lose its shape when washed and then need re-pressing. Most irons have a steam function and will produce different amounts of steam at different temperatures. Alternatively, spray the fabric with water using a spray bottle and then press it to create steam, or use a dampened pressing cloth.

My favorite pressing cloth is an old cotton tea towel with the hems cut off to prevent them making impressions on the fabric. A piece of silk organza can be a useful pressing cloth as its translucency enables you to see what you are doing, but it needs frequent dampening.

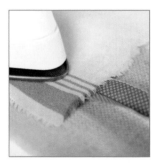
My favorite cotton pressing cloth.

An organza pressing cloth.

Pressing seams

"Press seam open" is a common instruction in sewing books and involves laying the fabric flat, opening out the seam allowances (see Sewing Straight Lines, page 30), and pressing them flat against the wrong side of the fabric.

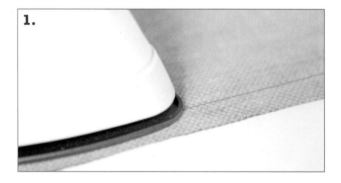

1 The first stage in pressing a seam open is to press it flat. Without opening out the fabric, press over the line of stitching you have just done to help the stitches sink into the fabric.

2 Then open the fabric out and lay it flat, right side down. Open out the seam allowances and press them flat. Turn the fabric over and check that the edges of the allowances haven't made an imprint on the fabric. If they have, then you need to slip strips of paper under the seam allowances and press them again.

Tailor's ham

This is a small, very firm cushion that you can lay a curved seam over (see Inward Curve and Outward Curve, pages 68–69) so that you can press it open without pressing it flat at the same time. It's a really useful piece of equipment. You can buy a ham, but it's easy to make your own.

1 Lay your iron on a piece of dressmaking cotton fabric and draw around it. Curve out the sides a little and round off the corners to make a classic ham shape, then add 2'' (5cm) all around.

2 Cut out the shape and use this as a template to cut the same shape once in woolen fabric and twice in thick cotton. Lay out a thick cotton ham shape with the dressmaking cotton shape face up on top of it, then the woolen shape face down and finally the other thick cotton shape. Pin the layers together.

3 Set the sewing machine to a medium straight stitch. Taking a ⅜'' (1cm) seam allowance, machine around the edges, leaving a 4'' (10cm) gap.

4 Turn the ham right side out through the gap. Fill it with sawdust (the type sold as bedding for hamsters is ideal), spooning it through the gap. You need to stuff the ham very firmly indeed, so use the spoon to press the sawdust down inside the ham so that you can force in as much as possible.

5 Hand-sew the gap closed using oversewing stitch to complete the ham. If after a few weeks the sawdust has compacted and the ham feels a bit soft, then you'll need to unpick the gap and push more sawdust in.

6 Lay a curved seam over the ham and press it open. Having one side of the ham in wool and one side in cotton allows you to use a high heat on the cotton side if it's needed.

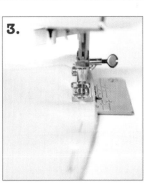

1.

2.

3.

4.

5.

6.

Pressing sleeves

You can make or buy a sleeve roll, which is a sausage-shaped version of a tailor's ham, but I prefer to use a towel because it can be made to fit any size or length of sleeve.

Roll the towel up so that it slides inside the sleeve, filling it without stretching it. You can now press the sleeve seam open without pressing the sleeve flat. This is also useful when you're ironing if you don't want pressed lines running down your sleeves.

Seams simple

The first and simplest sewing technique to learn is the seam. Once you can sew two pieces of fabric together, you can make something. There are different styles of seam and various ways of finishing the seam allowances, depending on what you are making and the fabric you use.

Sewing straight lines

Most often the seam you require will be straight, and it's important that you sew it straight. A wobbly seam will look terrible and can affect the fit of a garment. Many beginners struggle to sew in a straight line, but there are tips and tricks for mastering this, and of course I am going to share them with you. The amount of fabric between the raw, cut edge and the line of stitching that makes the seam is called the seam allowance. In dressmaking the standard seam allowance is ⅝'' (1.5cm), though you should always check a sewing pattern to see what it requires.

Check out...
Sewing tools and equipment, pages 16–17
How to run a sewing machine, page 21
Stitches, page 23

Plate marks

To help you keep to a straight line when sewing fabric, you can use one of four easy methods. Firstly, on the throat plate of the sewing machine there will be lines at marked distances from the needle, when it is in its usual sewing position. Usually these lines will be at ⅜'' (1cm), ⅝'' (1.5cm), and ¾'' (2cm) from the needle. If you keep the edge of the fabric running along the relevant marked line, the line of stitching will be that distance from the edge, giving you a seam allowance of that width.

Magnetic guide

To make this easier still, you can buy a magnetic seam guide. This is a handy little gadget that you put on the throat plate along the appropriate marked line. It gives you a raised, easy-to-see guide to keep the edge of the fabric running against while you sew the seam.

Masking tape

If you have to sew with a seam allowance that is wider than any of the marks on the throat plate, then stick a piece of masking tape on the bed of the machine to act as a guide. Measure out the required extra distance from the last marked line on the throat plate then stick on the tape, being careful to keep it parallel to the marked line.

Straight lines

Before you start sewing fabric, get some sheets of ruled paper (pages from an ordinary notebook are perfect) and practice sewing along the lines. Set the sewing machine to a medium straight stitch, take it slowly, pressing the foot pedal gently, and get used to guiding the paper with your hands to keep the line of sewing running along a line on the paper.

Before you start sewing fabric you MUST change the needle in the sewing machine because sewing the paper will have made it blunt.

Marked line

A completely different way of keeping to a seam line is to mark it on the fabric. Always use a proper fabric marker and test it on a scrap of the fabric first to make sure that you can remove the mark. This method can be useful when sewing a shaped seam, as you can concentrate on the stitching and not worry about where the edge of the fabric is.

Starting and finishing sewing

You need to secure the ends of all lines of stitching or they will work loose and your seams will split. There are two simple ways of doing this.

Check out...
Stitches, page 23
How to run a sewing machine, page 21
Sewing straight lines, page 30

Reverse stitching

Most modern sewing machines have a reverse stitch function. This is usually a little lever that you hold down, or a button you push, to make the machine sew backward, and a few backward stitches are a great way to secure the ends of most seams.

Position the fabric in the machine with the raw edges against the appropriate seam allowance mark and so that the needle will start sewing about ⅜" (1cm) from the start of the seam. You can check that the fabric is positioned correctly by turning the handwheel to lower the needle until it just touches the fabric. Hold down the reverse lever and slowly sew a few stitches backward. Try not to sew over the edge of the fabric as it may pucker.

Release the reverse lever and machine-sew forward to sew the seam. When you reach the other end of the seam, just before you get to the edge of the fabric, hold down the lever again and sew backward for ⅜" (1cm).

Knotting ends

If the line of stitching is visible (for example, top stitching), a reversed end can look untidy. The best solution here is to tie the threads in a firm knot on the wrong side of the fabric.

1 Before starting to sew, pull the top and bobbin threads through the machine until they are about 4" (10cm) long. Then sew the seam. At the other end, cut the threads 4" (10cm) from the fabric. Pull gently on the bobbin thread to pull a loop of the top thread down through the fabric. Slip a pin into this loop and pull the top thread right through, so that both ends of thread are on the wrong side of the fabric.

2 Tie a single knot, but take one end of the thread twice through the loop formed by the other end before tightening the knot. Tie a second knot in the usual way. This is called a surgeon's knot and the double twist at the start prevents the first knot slipping loose while you tie the second one. Trim the ends of the thread about ⅜" (1cm) from the knot.

3 If the knot is going to come under strain, sew in the ends of the threads. Thread the ends into a hand-sewing needle and either weave the needle in and out of a few stitches, or make tiny backstitches in the seam allowance, as shown. When weaving in and out of stitches, be careful to take the needle under them and not split the stitches with the tip of the needle.

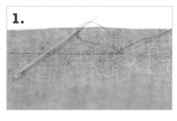
1.

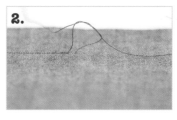
2.

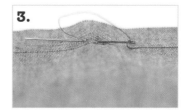
3.

Above: a line of stitching secured by reversed stitches (top) and by knotted and sewn in threads (below).

Finishing edges

Most fabrics will fray to some degree, so the raw, cut edges of an open seam allowance need to be neatened—or finished as it's also called—to prevent them eventually fraying so far that the seam splits. The method of finishing you choose will depend on how much your fabric frays, how special the project is, whether the seam allowances are visible, and whether they will be subject to wear and tear.

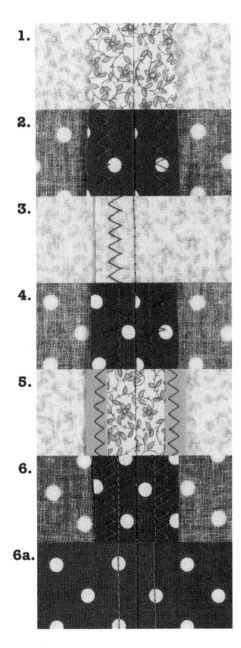

1.

2.

3.

4.

5.

6.

6a.

Check out...

Stitches, page 23

How to run a sewing machine,
   page 21

Pressing, pages 26-27

Sewing straight lines, page 30

Open seam, page 34

Zigzag bias binding, page 78

Best used for...

Open seams

All fabrics that fray

1 Items such as fancydress costumes or pillows made from fabric that doesn't fray much, can just have their seam allowances trimmed with pinking shears. This is perfectly adequate for projects that don't need to last or won't get much wear, but not for anything else.

2 The most commonly used method of finishing seam allowances is zigzagging them. All but the most ancient of sewing machines will have a zigzag function. Test the width and tightness of the zigzag on a scrap of the project fabric and adjust it until it fits within the seam allowance and doesn't pucker the fabric. Press the seam open then zigzag stitch along each allowance in turn. Trim them afterward if necessary.

3 If you are in a hurry and the project isn't special, then you can zigzag the allowances together. Press the seam open, then press it flat again. Set up the zigzag stitch as before, then zigzag stitch along both allowances together. Trim them if necessary, then press them to one side.

4 If your machine has an overcasting function, then you can use that to finish the allowances in a similar way to zigzagging.

5 For seams that will be visible, zigzag binding is practical and good-looking, though it is time consuming. If you can cut fabric and sew seams very accurately, then consider binding all the edges of the project pieces before sewing them together; it's easier, but hard to change if you get anything wrong. Otherwise, bind the seam allowances after sewing the seam. Turn to Zigzag Bias Binding (page 78) for instructions.

6 Pinked, open zigzagged, overcast, and bound seams can be topstitched for added security, and the lines of stitching are a great finishing detail on the right side (see 6a.). This is practical for thick fabrics, or fabrics that are difficult to press so the seam allowances don't lie very flat.

Finish the seam allowances using the desired method. Right side up, place the fabric under the machine with the edge of the presser foot against the seam. Keeping the edge of the foot against the seam so the stitching is beautifully straight, topstitch the length of the seam, sewing through the main fabric and seam allowance.

Repeat on the other side of the seam, starting from the same end as before. Working in the same direction on each side of the seam prevents the fabric distorting.

You can topstitch seam allowances that have been zigzagged together with a single line of top stitching on one side of the seam. However, this can make for a bulky seam, so experiment on a scrap of the fabric first.

Trimming and layering seams

If a seam is joining more than two layers of fabric, or if a fabric is very thick, the seam can become bulky. This can make it lie badly or show on the right side of the fabric when the seam is pressed. Trimming the seam allowances can cure these problems.

Check out...

Pressing, pages 26–27
Sewing straight lines, page 30
Finishing edges, page 32
Open seam, page 34

Best used for...

Open seams
All fabrics, especially
heavyweight ones

Trimming

When two layers of thick fabric are seamed, carefully trim off up to two-thirds of one or both seam allowances using small scissors. Trimming one seam allowance only will mean that the two no longer align and so will produce less of a bump if they are pressed to the same side. Trimming both seam allowances makes the seam less bulky if it is being pressed open. If you are concerned about the fabric fraying, either trim with pinking shears or finish the edge after trimming it.

Above: seam allowances with one allowance trimmed and both zigzagged.

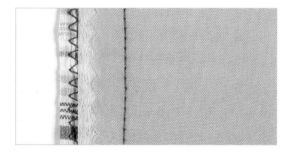

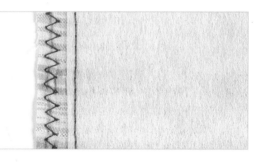

Layering

If there are several layers of fabric in a seam, then trim them to different depths. Above, the seam allowance of the main fabric (the striped fabric) has been left the full width. The interfacing has been trimmed to about ⅜" (1cm) and the lining to about ¼" (5mm). The edge of the main fabric could be finished by zigzagging or overcasting; the interfacing won't fray so it can be left as it is; and the lining is trimmed with pinking shears as it would be tricky to finish such a narrow seam allowance in any other way.

If the fabric is interfaced with sew-in interfacing, as above, then that can be trimmed very close to the line of stitching as it won't fray. If you are using iron-on interfacing, then trim it before ironing it onto the fabric and sewing the seam.

Shaped seams

These also need to be trimmed, but in slightly different ways depending on whether they are corners, curves, or points. Turn to Around The Corner (pages 64–71) to find out how to deal with the seam allowances on these shapes.

Open seam

This is the most basic seam and the one that you will use most often. Although it's easy to do, it's worth learning to sew it smoothly and well, as all of your projects will look better when the seams are perfect.

Check out...

Stitches, page 23
How to run a sewing machine,
    page 21
Pinning, page 24
Basting, page 25
Pressing, pages 26-27
Sewing straight lines, page 30
Starting and finishing sewing,
    page 31
Finishing edges, page 32

Best used for...

Straight seams
Gently curved seams
All fabrics, especially
    heavyweight ones

1 Right sides together, pin the two pieces to be seamed and, if necessary, baste them ⅜" (1cm) from the raw edges.

2 Set the sewing machine to a medium straight stitch. Position the fabric in the sewing machine to take a ⅝" (1.5cm) seam allowance. If the ends of the seam are going to be reversed to secure the stitching, position the fabric so that the needle will start sewing about ⅜" (1cm) from the start of the seam.

Left: an open seam on the right side of the project (above) and on the wrong side (below).

3 Sew in reverse for ⅜" (1cm), then machine-sew forward to sew the seam. When you reach the other end, sew in reverse for ⅜" (1cm).

4 Remove the basting stitches. Press the seamed area flat, then press the seam allowances open. Finish the edges of the seam allowances as desired.

Mock French seam

Easier to sew than a traditional French seam, a mock French seam completely encloses the raw edges of the fabric, giving a beautifully neat finish on the reverse. Don't use it for heavyweight fabrics as the result will be both bulky and stiff. This seam, the French Seam (page 36), and Self-bound Seam (page 37), all have a little ridge on the inside that's made by the enclosed seam allowances, so these seams are not great for tight-fitting garments.

Check out...
Stitches, page 23
How to run a sewing machine, page 21
Pinning, page 24
Basting, page 25
Pressing, pages 26–27
Sewing straight lines, page 30
Starting and finishing sewing, page 31
Open seam, page 34

Best used for...
Straight seams
Gently curved seams
Sheer, lightweight, and mediumweight fabrics
Seams where the reverse is visible
Seams where the reverse will be subject to wear and tear

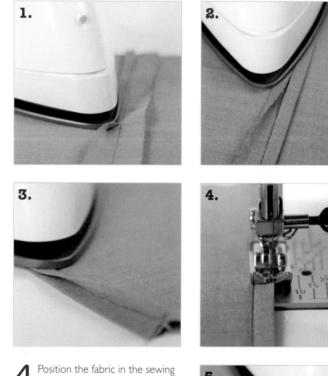

1 Sew the pieces together following Steps 1–4 of Open Seam, but do not finish the seam allowances. Fold one of the pressed-open seam allowances in half so that the raw edge of the fabric just touches the line of stitching. Press the fold.

2 Fold in and press the other seam allowance in the same way.

3 Fold the fabric flat so that the right sides are together. Press the seamed area flat again, so that the folded edges of the seam allowances are touching.

4 Position the fabric in the sewing machine so that the needle will start sewing very close to the folded edges. You can check if the fabric is in the correct position by turning the handwheel to lower the needle until it just touches the fabric. Machine-sew the edges together, then knot the threads to secure them (it's quite tricky to reverse-stitch a seam so close to the edge).

5 Press the seamed area, then open the fabric out flat and press the enclosed seam allowance to one side.

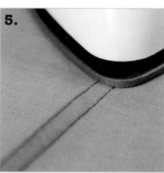

Right: a mock French seam on the right side of the project (above) and on the wrong side (below).

French seam

This is a classic seam that encloses the raw edges of the fabric to create a neat finish on both sides of the work. It's particularly good for sheer fabrics, such as the cotton organdie that is being used here, but not for fabrics that fray very easily. You need to be careful and accurate when trimming the allowances in Step 2 so that no stray threads poke out through the final line of stitching.

Check out...

Stitches, page 23
How to run a sewing machine, page 21
Pinning, page 24
Basting, page 25
Pressing, pages 26–27
Sewing straight lines, page 30
Starting and finishing sewing, page 31
Open seam, page 34

Best used for...

Straight seams
Sheer, lightweight, and mediumweight fabrics
Seams where the reverse is visible
Seams where the reverse will be subject to wear and tear

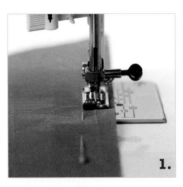

1.

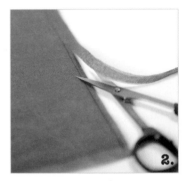

2.

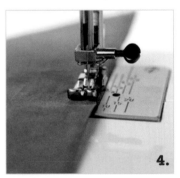

3.

4.

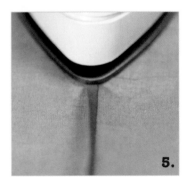

5.

1 Pin the pieces of fabric together with the WRONG SIDES facing each other. Sew the pieces together following Steps 1–3 of Open Seam, but taking a ⅜" (1cm) seam allowance. Press the seamed area flat, but do not press the seam allowances open.

2 Trim both of the seam allowances to approximately ⅛" (3mm).

3 Along the seam, fold the fabric so that the RIGHT SIDES are facing each other and the trimmed seam is hidden in the fold. Pin the layers together.

4 Put the fabric under the foot of the machine with the folded edge ¼" (5mm) from the needle. Many machines do not have a ¼" (5mm) mark on the throat plate, so either measure out from the needle and mark the distance with masking tape, or use a ¼" (5mm) presser foot, as here. Sew the seam, reversing at each end to secure the stitching.

5 Press the seamed area, then open the fabric out flat and press the enclosed seam allowance to one side.

Left: a French seam on the right side of the project (above) and on the wrong side (below).

Self-bound seam

Of all the seams with enclosed edges this is the best one for fabrics that fray easily, such as the dupioni silk used here, but don't use it for heavyweight fabrics. The reverse is not quite as attractive as that of the Mock French Seam (page 35) and French Seam (opposite), but it will be durable.

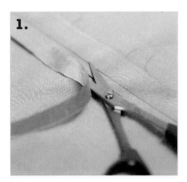

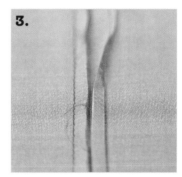

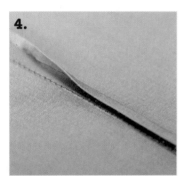

1 Sew the pieces together following Steps 1–4 of Open Seam, but do not finish the seam allowances. Trim one of the seam allowances to ¼" (5mm).

2 Press the trimmed allowance over so that it lies flat on top of the untrimmed allowance.

3 Fold over the edge of the untrimmed allowance until it almost, but not quite, touches the trimmed edge. Press the fold.

4 Fold the pressed edge over the trimmed edge so that the pressed fold lies along the line of stitching of the original seam. The fold shouldn't overlap the stitching or the seam can look lumpy on the right side.

5 Fold the fabric right sides together along the original seam and press the folded seam allowances. Position the fabric in the sewing machine so that the needle will start sewing very close to the folded edge: you can check this by turning the handwheel to lower the needle until it just touches the fabric. Machine-sew the seam. Press the seamed area, then open the fabric out flat and press the enclosed seam allowance to one side so that the folded-over edge is uppermost.

Check out...
Stitches, page 23
How to run a sewing machine, page 21
Pinning, page 24
Basting, page 25
Pressing, pages 26–27
Sewing straight lines, page 30
Starting and finishing sewing, page 31
Open seam, page 34

Best used for...
Straight seams
Lightweight and mediumweight fabrics
Fabrics that fray easily
Seams where the reverse will be subject to wear and tear

Right: a self-bound seam on the right side of the project (above) and on the wrong side (below).

Flat fell seam

Probably best known as the type of seam that runs down the outside leg of a pair of jeans, the flat fell seam is robust, suitable for heavyweight fabrics and, unlike all the other enclosed seams, it is flat on the reverse and so very comfortable to wear. It does require a beautifully straight line of stitching to finish it in Step 5.

Check out...

Stitches, page 23
How to run a sewing machine, page 21
Pinning, page 24
Basting, page 25
Pressing, pages 26–27
Sewing straight lines, page 30
Starting and finishing sewing, page 31
Open seam, page 34

Best used for...

Straight seams
Mediumweight and heavyweight fabrics
Seams where the reverse will be subject to wear and tear

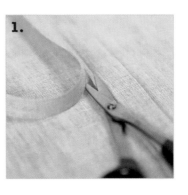

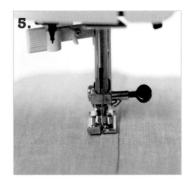

1 Pin the pieces of fabric together with the WRONG SIDES facing each other. Sew the pieces together following Steps 1–4 of Open Seam, but do not finish the seam allowances. Trim one of the seam allowances to ¼" (5mm).

2 Press the trimmed allowance over so that it lies flat on top of the untrimmed allowance.

Left: a flat fell seam on the right side of the project (above) and on the wrong side (below).

3 Fold over the edge of the untrimmed allowance so that it touches the trimmed edge. Press the fold.

4 Press the whole of the untrimmed allowance over so that it covers the trimmed one and all the raw edges are hidden.

5 Position the fabric in the sewing machine so that the needle will start sewing very close to the folded edge. You can check that the fabric is in the right position by turning the handwheel to lower the needle until it just touches the fabric. Machine-sew very close to the

folded edge to complete the seam. Press the seam flat.

Intersecting seams

Seams that cross or meet need to be treated in a particular way to avoid lumps of stacked seam allowances. This sample shows seams crossing one another, but the same principles apply if two seams form a T-shape.

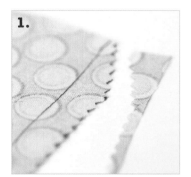

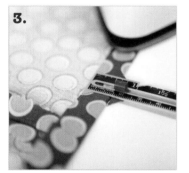

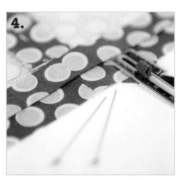

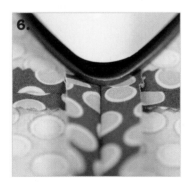

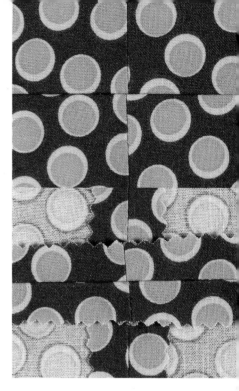

Right: intersecting seams on the right side of the project (above) and on the wrong side (below).

1 Sew the first pieces together following Steps 1–3 of Open Seam. Press the seamed area flat, but do not press the seam allowances open. At the end of the seam that will intersect, trim the seam allowances to a point, starting to cut about ¾" (2cm) from the end of the seam and sloping the cut to end about ⅛" (3mm) from the line of stitching. Trimming the seam allowance with pinking shears will help prevent fraying without adding bulk.

2 Press the seam allowances open. Repeat Steps 1–2 on the other intersecting piece.

3 Measuring accurately, press under the seam allowance (across the trimmed end of the first seam) on one of the pieces to be joined.

4 Lay the pressed piece on the other piece, ⅝" (1.5cm) from the raw edge, and match up the seams perfectly. Pin the pieces together, then press the top seam allowance flat again.

5 Taking a ⅝" (1.5cm) seam allowance, sew the new seam as for an Open Seam. Stitch carefully over the ends of the first seams, being sure not to ruck up or pucker the seam allowances.

6 Press the new seam flat, then press it open.

Check out...

Stitches, page 23

How to run a sewing machine, page 21

Pinning, page 24

Basting, page 25

Pressing, pages 26–27

Sewing straight lines, page 30

Starting and finishing sewing, page 31

Open seam, page 34

Best used for...

Lightweight and mediumweight fabrics

Hemmed in

Many of your sewing projects will need a hem somewhere, whether it's the lower edge of a skirt, the top edge of a bag, or the opening of a pillowcase. A smooth, beautifully stitched hem of the right type for the project will help give your work that finish that carries it over the line from homemade into handmade.

Hem allowance

The amount of fabric folded over to make the hem is called the hem allowance. On lightweight fabrics this is usually 1" (2.5cm) for a single hem and for a double hem—the most commonly used type—it will usually be 1⅜" (3.5cm). Always check a pattern to see what it specifies.

Hem allowances on heavier fabrics can be up to 3" (8cm), as narrow hems on thick fabrics become stiff and bulky. Curtains will routinely have a hem allowance of up to 8" (20cm).

You can add extra to the hem allowance on children's garments to allow for letting the hem down as they grow, but bear in mind that too deep a hem will hang oddly. When the hem is let down there may be a permanent mark on the fabric along the original fold line. This mark can be disguised by sewing ribbon or braid over it (see Sewing On Ribbon Or Braid, page 90), but a fashion-conscious child may not be thrilled by this idea.

Single hem

Above: a single hem on the right side of the project (left) and on the wrong side (right).

This is the most basic of hems and is only suitable if either the edge being turned up is the selvage, or if the project doesn't need to wear well—a Halloween outfit maybe—and the raw edge can be zigzagged. Selvages are tempting to use, but can cause problems so read the box below before using such an edge.

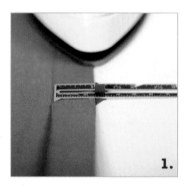

1.

2.

Check out...
Stitches, page 23
How to run a sewing machine, page 21
Pinning, page 24
Pressing, pages 26–27
Starting and finishing sewing, page 31

Best used for...
Straight hems
Selvage edges
All fabrics

1 Using a ruler or seam gauge to check the measurement right along the hem, fold the selvage edge of the fabric over by 1" (2.5cm). Press the fold.

2 Pin the selvage edge in place. Set the sewing machine to a medium straight stitch. Put the fabric under the presser foot of the machine with the edge of the foot against the selvage edge. Machine-sew the hem, removing pins as you get to them and reversing at each end to secure the stitching.

Selvages

The selvage is the edge along the length of the fabric: it is created during production of the fabric and won't fray. Woven fabrics, such as the one used here, usually have a selvage that is the same colour as the main part of the fabric, but it can have a slightly different, tighter weave. This can shrink during washing, which would make a selvage-edge hem pucker unattractively and permanently. Printed fabrics usually have a white selvage—often with the manufacturer's name printed on it—and that, too, can be of a different weave. If you want to use a selvage, wash a bit of the fabric first to see what happens.

Double hem

Above: a double hem on the right side of the project (left) and on the wrong side (right).

The most commonly used type of hem, this gives a neat finish by enclosing the raw edge. If the fabric frays readily, then either trim the raw edge with pinking shears or zigzag it before making the first fold.

Check out...

Stitches, page 23

How to run a sewing machine, page 21

Pinning, page 24

Basting, page 25

Pressing, pages 26–27

Starting and finishing sewing, page 31

Finishing edges, page 32

Single hem, page 42

1 Using a ruler or seam gauge to check the measurement right along the hem, fold the edge of the fabric over by ⅜″ (1cm). Press the fold.

2 Fold the fabric over by a further 1″ (2.5cm) and press this second fold. Pin the folded edge in place and machine-sew the hem as for a Single Hem, positioning the edge of the foot against the first pressed fold.

Best used for...

Straight hems

All fabrics

Narrow hem

It can be difficult to make a very narrow double hem, especially on sheer fabrics. This method is quick, easy, and successful. You need a hem allowance the desired width of the double hem, plus ⅝″ (1.5cm).

Check out...

Stitches, page 23

How to run a sewing machine, page 21

Pinning, page 24

Basting, page 25

Pressing, pages 26–27

Starting and finishing sewing, page 31

Double hem, page 43

1 Using a ruler or seam gauge to check the measurement right along the hem, fold the edge of the fabric over by ⅝″ (1.5cm) and pin in place. Set the sewing machine to a medium straight stitch and machine-sew along the folded edge, sewing very close to the fold.

2 Trim the seam allowance close to the line of stitching. The distance between the folded edge and the trimmed edge establishes the depth of the hem.

3 Fold the hem over to enclose the raw edge and machine sew again, sewing over the first line of stitching to complete the hem.

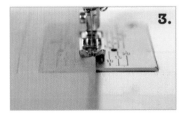

Best used for...

Straight hems

Sheer and lightweight fabrics

Below: a narrow hem on the right side of the project (left) and on the wrong side (right).

Blind-stitch hem

Above: a blind-stitch hem on the right side of the project (left) and on the wrong side (right).

This is a hem that relies on your sewing machine having a blind stitch setting, but it is a fairly basic function and most modern machines will have it. It can require a bit of fiddling about to get a perfect result, so check the instruction manual for your sewing machine for any specific information and practice on a spare piece of the fabric first before hemming a project.

Check out...

Stitches, page 17
How to run a sewing machine, page 23
Pinning, page 24
Basting, page 25
Pressing, pages 26–27
Starting and finishing sewing, page 31
Finishing edges, page 32
Double hem, page 43

Best used for...

Straight hems
All fabrics

1.

2.

3.

4.

1 Follow Steps 1–2 of Double Hem.

2 Fold the pressed hem to the right side of the main fabric so that just a small amount of the ⅜" (1cm) hem is visible, as shown. The precise amount that needs to be visible will depend on the settings your sewing machine uses, so this is where the manual and practice come in.

3 Set the sewing machine to the blind stitch setting and fit the correct presser foot (this will usually be a zigzag foot or a special blind-hem foot). Turn the handwheel until the needle is at the furthest right position and then put the fabric in the machine so that the needle goes into the visible section of the folded-under hem.

4 As you sew the hem, the needle will move across to the left and at its furthest left position it should be going down into the fabric just over the folded-back edge. The needle should not be right on the fold or the stitch will not catch enough of the fabric to make the hem secure. It also should not be too far over the fold or the stitch will be very visible on the right side. Experiment on your spare piece of fabric until you've got the position of the fabric under the needle exactly right, then, if necessary, mark the position of the right-hand edge of the fabric on the throat plate with a piece of masking tape.

Curved hem

Above: a curved hem on the right side of the project (left) and on the wrong side (right).

Projects with curved edges—such as a circular skirt or a round tablecloth—will need this hemming technique. The basting might seem a little time-consuming, but it is worth doing for a perfect finish. Remember to test the fabric marker on a scrap of the fabric to make sure the mark will disappear.

1.

2.

3.

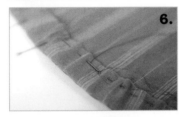
4.

5.

6.

7.

Check out...

Stitches, page 23

How to run a sewing machine, page 21

Pinning, page 24

Basting, page 25

Pressing, pages 26–27

Starting and finishing sewing, page 31

Finishing edges, page 32

Double hem, page 43

Best used for...

All fabrics

1 Using a ruler or seam gauge to measure accurately, mark concentric lines 1⅜" (3.5cm) and ⅜" (1cm) in from the edge of the fabric. The best way to do this is to make a line of marks 2" (5cm) apart, then join them freehand.

2 Using a contrast-colored thread, baste along both marked lines. You can use quite long basting stitches, but try to make them fairly even in length. Leave long tails of thread at each end of the basted line nearest the raw edge.

3 Fold the fabric over along this lower basted line and press the fold. Don't worry about pressing any puckers or gathers in the folded-over fabric, just concentrate on getting a smooth hem line.

4 Fold the fabric over along the upper basted line, but do not press the fold at this stage. Put in lots of vertical pins—heads facing out—to hold the hem in position. Again, don't worry about puckers in the fabric, concentrate on making the hem line a smooth curve.

5 Gently pull on the long tails of thread left at each end of the lower basted line. Working methodically along the hem, pull up and adjust the gathers evenly until the inner edge lies as flat as possible.

6 Baste along the inner edge of the hem, using small stitches to baste the gathers in place. Press the hem, pressing the gathers flat.

7 Set the sewing machine to a medium straight stitch. Put the fabric under the machine with the edge of the foot against the inner hem line. Machine-sew the hem, sewing carefully over the gathers to prevent them pushing up into lumpy groups. Remove the basting stitches and press the finished hem thoroughly.

Corner hem

The idea of having to produce a square, flat, mitered corner is one that sends many novice sewers pale, but it isn't a difficult technique to get right, you just need to be able to measure and press accurately. As usual, the raw edges can be overcast or zigzagged if you are worried about the fabric fraying.

Check out...

Stitches, page 23

How to run a sewing machine, page 21

Pinning, page 24

Basting, page 25

Pressing, pages 26–27

Starting and finishing sewing, page 31

Finishing edges, page 32

Double hem, page 43

Inward square corner, page 66

Best used for...

All fabrics

1.

2.

3.

1 Using a ruler or seam gauge to measure accurately, fold the edges of the fabric over by ⅜" (1cm) and press the folds. Fold the edges over by another 1" (2.5cm) and press these second folds.

2 Open the pressed hems out flat and lay the fabric right side down. At the corner, fold over a triangle of fabric: the point where the second pressed lines cross should be in the middle of the folded-over edge. Press the corner fold flat.

3 Open the corner out then, right sides together, fold the corner in half, matching the raw edges and the ends of the pressed corner fold. Pin the layers together along the pressed corner fold, with the head of the pin facing toward the raw edges of the fabric.

Left: a corner hem on the right side of the project. Right: and on the wrong side.

4.

5.

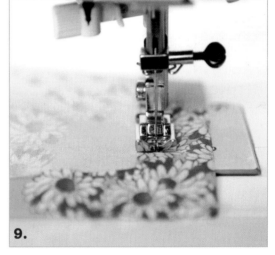
6.

7.

8.

9.

4 Set the sewing machine to a medium straight stitch. Starting at the fold, machine-sew along the pressed corner line as far as the first pressed hem line, reversing at each end to secure the stitching.

5 Trim off the corner of fabric ¼" (5mm) above the line of stitching. At the folded edge, clip off a little more fabric at an angle, as shown.

6 Open the corner out square along the second pressed hem lines. Press the edge trimmed in Step 5 to one side. The clipped angle—which is now at the point—should sit neatly inside the square corner.

7 Turn the corner right side out and re-press the second hem lines so that everything lies square and flat.

8 Turn under the first pressed hem lines and pin them in place.

9 Put the fabric under the machine with the edge of the foot against the first hem line. Machine-sew the hem, pivoting the fabric around the needle at the square corner. Press the hemmed edges and corner thoroughly.

Taped hem

Above: a slip-stitched taped hem on the right side of the project (left) and on the wrong side (right).

If you don't have enough fabric for a double hem (maybe because you are letting a garment down), then a taped hem is a great solution. It's also good for very heavy fabrics where a double hem would be very bulky. This example uses a lightweight fabric and ribbon, but for heavyweight fabrics you should use purpose-made hem tape. Before sewing on the ribbon, zigzag the raw edge of the fabric if it frays easily.

Check out...

Stitches, page 23
How to run a sewing machine, page 21
Pinning, page 24
Basting, page 25
Pressing, pages 26–27
Starting and finishing sewing, page 31
Finishing edges, page 32
Single hem, page 42
Faced hem, page 49

Best used for...

Straight hems
All fabrics, particularly
  heavyweight ones

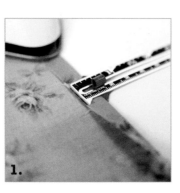

1.

2.

3.

4.

1 Using a ruler or seam gauge to check the measurement right along the hem, fold the edge of the fabric over by ⅜'' (1cm). Press the fold.

2 Lay the fabric flat and pin the ribbon to the right side, ¼'' (5mm) below the fold.

3 Set the sewing machine to a medium straight stitch. Put the fabric under the presser foot of the machine with the edge of the foot against the pressed fold: when you start sewing the line of stitching should be on the ribbon, very close to the upper edge. Machine-sew the ribbon to the fabric.

4 Re-fold the fabric along the line pressed in Step 1, then you have a choice of finishing technique. You can machine-sew along the other edge of the ribbon or you can slipstitch it by hand, as shown. Slip stitching is almost invisible on the right side, but if you machine-sew the edge then the line of stitching will be visible (see Step 6, Faced Hem, opposite).

Choosing ribbon or tape

The ribbon or tape must be a similar weight to the fabric, so don't use lightweight ribbon on thick woolen fabric. Also, you must take laundering into account: the ribbon and the fabric must be wash-compatible. Once you've resolved these practical issues, consider the look of the thing. A pretty, patterned tape will be seen by almost no-one except you, but you'll know it's there. It adds a fabulous finishing touch, and those who do catch a glimpse will be impressed.

Faced hem

This style of hem is similar to the Taped Hem and is great if you are short of your main fabric, but as you are joining two fabrics close to the hem line it's not good for heavyweight fabrics because the seam will create bulk. Again, it's a perfect opportunity to add a designerly touch to a project by facing the hem in a fabric that complements—or contrasts with—the main fabric. The facing should be between 2¾" (7cm) and 1½" (4cm) deep and should be of a fabric that is a similar weight and fiber content as the main fabric. The technique is shown here on a straight hem, but you can also use it on curved hems, just cut the facing to match the curve of the main fabric.

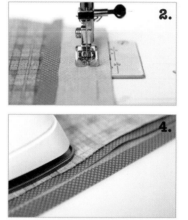

1 Cut a facing the required depth plus 1¼" (3cm) for hem and seam allowances. Turn under and press a ⅝" (1.5cm) hem along the upper edge of the facing. Right sides together and matching the raw edges, pin the facing to the main fabric.

2 Set the sewing machine to a medium straight stitch. Using thread to match the facing and taking a ⅝" (1.5cm) seam allowance, machine-sew the facing to the hem.

3 Trim the seam allowance of the main fabric to about half its depth. This edge can be cut with pinking shears if the fabric has a tendency to fray.

4 Press the seam flat then press the facing flat, pressing both seam allowances toward the facing.

5 Understitch the facing by sewing a line of machine stitching ⅛" (3mm) from the seamline, sewing through both seam allowances and the facing.

6 Fold the facing to the wrong side of the main fabric, folding over just a tiny amount of the main fabric at the same time to ensure that none of the facing shows on the right side. Press the fold. You can finish the top edge as for a Taped Hem by either slipstitching or machine-sewing it. If you slipstitch then choose a thread color to match the main fabric. If you machine sew, then sew with the facing uppermost and match the spool thread to the facing and the bobbin thread to the main fabric for best results.

Check out...

Stitches, page 23

How to run a sewing machine, page 21

Pinning, page 24

Basting, page 25

Pressing, pages 26–27

Starting and finishing sewing, page 31

Finishing edges, page 32

Taped hem, page 48

Best used for...

Straight and curved hems

Lightweight and mediumweight fabrics

Fastened up

Zippers, buttonholes, ties, and loops are all fastenings you'll want to use in your sewing projects. There are tips and tricks for inserting and making them that will make the tasks easier and the end results look better.

Centered zipper

This style of zipper is typically used to fasten a skirt or pants. Zippers can seem daunting, but if you follow these instructions carefully you'll find it easy to insert one. The technique is exactly the same for the different types of zipper—concealed zipper, dress zipper, or metal-toothed zipper.

1.

2.

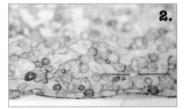
3.

4.

5.

6.

Check out...

Stitches, page 23

How to run a sewing machine, page 21

Pinning, page 24

Basting, page 25

Pressing, pages 26–27

Sewing straight lines, page 30

Starting and finishing sewing, page 31

Finishing edges, page 32

Open seam, page 34

Shortening a zipper, page 57

Best used for...

Zipper that opens at the top of a seam

1 Mark with a pin the position in the seam where the end of the zipper will be. Sew the seam up to the pin, take the pin out and reverse a few stitches to secure the end of the seam.

2 Using a fabric marker, mark the seamline on the open section of the seam, where the zipper will be. Baste along the marked seamline, using short, tight basting stitches to close the open section of the seam.

3 Press the whole seam—the machine-sewn section and the basted section—open. At this stage you should finish the edges of the seam allowances by either zigzagging or overcasting them.

4 With the fabric right side down, position the end stop of the zipper on the machine-sewn section of the seam, just below the start of the basting. Align the teeth with the seamline and pin the zipper in place through the tape. Lay the zipper along the basted section of the seam, keeping the teeth aligned with the seamline and pinning it in place.

5 Baste the zipper in position, basting through the zipper tape on both sides of the teeth. Baste in the middle of the tape to avoid getting entangled in the machine sewing.

6 When you are machine-sewing the zipper, you'll need to move the pull and on some zippers this is easier to do by pulling up than by pushing down. Test yours to see how easily the pull moves in each direction and if it is trickier to push down, then wriggle it down to the halfway point now, before you start sewing.

7 Set the sewing machine to a medium straight stitch and fit the zipper foot. Position the top of the zipper under the foot with the side of the foot against the zipper teeth, so that the needle will start sewing as close to the teeth as possible. Sewing quite slowly, sew the zipper in place—keeping the edge of the zipper foot running along the teeth of the zipper—until just before you reach the pull.

8 Stop sewing with the needle down in the fabric. Lift the presser foot and wriggle the pull up past the needle. This can be a bit tricky and you may need to pivot the fabric around the needle, which is fine as long as the needle remains firmly in place in the fabric. Don't move the pull up to the top, just enough to get it past the needle. Straighten the fabric, lower the presser foot, and continue sewing to the bottom of the zipper, just below the end stop.

9 Sew across the zipper tape below the end stop. Cut and knot the threads to secure the stitching.

10 Move the zipper foot to the other side. Starting at the top of the zipper, repeat Steps 7–8 to sew the other side of the zipper tape in place, knotting the threads at the bottom to secure the stitching. Sewing from the top down on both sides of the zipper prevents the fabric twisting.

11 Using sharp embroidery scissors and the tip of a darning needle, cut and pull the basting stitches out of the seam. Press the fabric flat over the zipper.

Zipper trick

If you are making a skirt or pants with a waistband and a centered or lapped zipper, then buy a zipper that is about 2" (5cm) longer than you need. Prepare the seam and position the zipper end stop as usual. Pin the zipper in place so that the top, and the pull, protrude above the edge of the fabric. Sew the zipper in place quickly and easily, without having to wriggle the pull past the needle. Unpick the basting, open the zipper, cut the protruding top section off and sew the waistband over the teeth at the top of the zipper. So simple and clever.

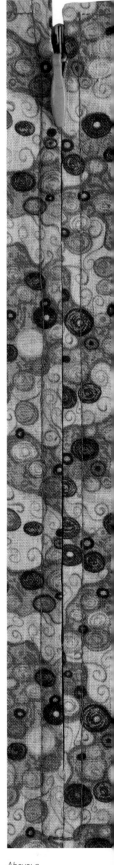

Above: a centered zipper.

Inset zipper

You'll use this zipper in the middle of a seam, perhaps in the side seam of a dress or across the back of a large pillow. The principle is very similar to a centered zipper.

Check out...
Stitches, page 23
How to run a sewing machine, page 21
Pinning, page 24
Basting, page 25
Pressing, pages 26–27
Sewing straight lines, page 30
Starting and finishing sewing, page 31
Finishing edges, page 32
Open seam, page 34
Shortening a zipper, page 57
Centered zipper, pages 52–53

Best used for...
Zipper that opens in the middle of a seam

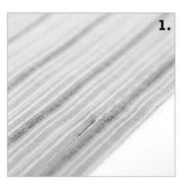

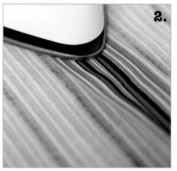

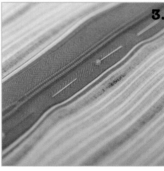

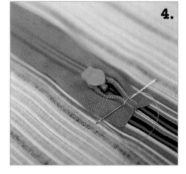

1 Follow Steps 1–2 of Centered Zipper, putting in a pin to mark both ends of the zipper and sewing both ends of the seam. Baste the open center section.

2 Press the whole seam—the machine-sewn section and the basted section—open. At this stage you should finish the edges of the seam allowances by either zigzagging or overcasting them.

3 Follow Steps 4–6 of Centered Zipper to pin then baste the zipper in position.

4 At the top of the zipper, baste the toothless section of the tape together above the zipper pull.

5 Follow Steps 7–11 of Centered Zipper to machine-sew the zipper in place and finish it. Machine-sew across the basted tape at the top, down one side, and across the end. Then sew down the other side, starting from the top.

Left: an inset zipper.

Separating zipper

This is the type of zipper typically used on a jacket; the two halves separate completely at the bottom. Nylon zippers of this style are usually available in just a narrow range of colors, with the metal-toothed ones being more easily found.

Check out...

Stitches, page 23

How to run a sewing machine,
    page 21

Pinning, page 24

Basting, page 25

Pressing, pages 26-27

Starting and finishing sewing,
    page 31

Finishing edges, page 32

Centered zipper, pages 52-53

Best used for...

Zipper that needs to
    open completely

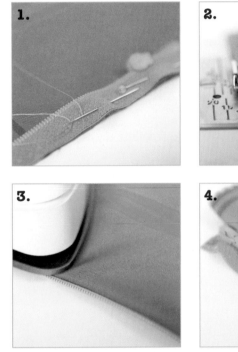

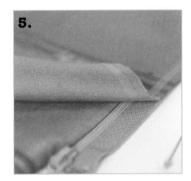

1 Finish the edges of the fabric before you insert the zipper. Separate the zipper and lay the side with the pull right side down on the right side of one piece of fabric. Match the edge of the zipper tape with the raw edge of the fabric. Pin then baste this side of the zipper in position.

2 Follow Steps 7–8 of Centered Zipper to machine-sew the zipper in place. Knot the threads at the back at each end.

3 Fold the zipper tape to the wrong side of the fabric, so that only the teeth show on the right side. Press the fold.

4 Zip the free side of the zipper onto the sewn-on side.

5 With the zipper flat and right side up, lay the other piece of fabric right side down on top of it. Match the raw edge of the fabric with the edge of the zipper tape and pin then baste them together.

6 Separate the zipper again. Machine-sew, then fold and press the second side of the zipper in place in the same way as for the first side. Remove all basting stitches.

Right: a separating zipper. You can topstitch the fabric close to the zipper teeth to help hold the zipper tape flat; the left-hand side of this sample has been topstitched.

Lapped zipper

As with a centered zipper, this style is used for skirts and pants, but it's more professional-looking as a flap of fabric completely covers the zipper. There are some complicated ways of inserting this style of zipper, but this method is straightforward. You may find that you prefer it—as I do—to a centered zipper for looks and ease of insertion. In this example the overlap is on the right-hand side, so the zipper would be on the left-hand side of the body.

Check out...

Stitches, page 23
How to run a sewing machine, page 21
Pinning, page 24
Basting, page 25
Pressing, pages 26–27
Sewing straight lines, page 30
Starting and finishing sewing, page 31
Finishing edges, page 32
Open seam, page 34
Centered zipper, pages 52–53

Best used for...

Zipper that opens at the top of a seam

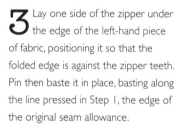
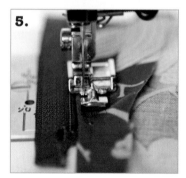
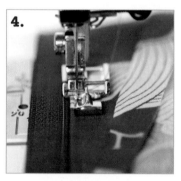

1 Follow Step 1 of Centered Zipper to sew the seam below where the zipper will be. Using a seam gauge to measure accurately, press the ⅝'' (1.5cm) allowances on the open section of the seam to the wrong side. Finish the seam allowances by zigzagging or overcasting them.

2 Lay the fabric right side up with the open end of the seam toward you. Open the left-hand seam allowance out and then re-press ⅜'' (1cm) to the wrong side. On the right side you'll see the original pressed line then a further ¼'' (5mm) of fabric.

Right: a lapped zipper.

3 Lay one side of the zipper under the edge of the left-hand piece of fabric, positioning it so that the folded edge is against the zipper teeth. Pin then baste it in place, basting along the line pressed in Step 1, the edge of the original seam allowance.

4 Set the sewing machine to a medium straight stitch and fit the zipper foot. Right side up, position the top of the zipper under the foot with the side of the foot against the zipper teeth, so that the needle will start sewing as close to the teeth as possible. Have the right-hand piece of fabric folded right side down across the side you are sewing. Machine-sew the basted side of the zipper in place.

5 As you get toward the bottom of the zipper, make sure the right-hand piece of fabric is completely out of the way so that you can sew past the start of the seam to sew the tape to the seam allowance right down to the bottom of the zipper.

6 With the fabric right side up, lay the right-hand piece over the zipper, matching the folded edge with the line on the left-hand side that was pressed in Step 1. Pin the flap in place.

7 Turn the fabric over. On the wrong side, baste the free side of the zipper tape to the fabric. Keep the stitches in a straight line, as they will be your guide when it comes to machine-sewing this side of the zipper.

8 Right side up, position the fabric under the foot so that the needle will start sewing along the line of basting stitches worked in Step 7. This is one occasion where you will be sewing over basting stitches and you'll need to pick them out afterward. Machine-sew from the top to the bottom of the zipper.

9 With the needle down in the fabric, lift the presser foot and pivot the fabric 90° around the needle. Sew across the bottom of the flap. Knot the threads on the back to secure the stitching. Remove all basting stitches.

Shortening a zipper

Sometimes you won't be able to get a zipper that's the right length, but for centered, inset, and lapped zippers it's very easy to shorten a longer one as needed. This technique works on all nylon-toothed zippers; for metal-toothed ones, follow Step 1, then use craft pliers to pull off a couple of the zipper teeth ⅜" (1cm) below the stitches so that you can cut the tape without damaging your shears.

Check out...
Centered zipper, pages 52–53
Inset zipper, page 54
Lapped zipper, pages 56–57

Best used for...
Centered, inset, and
   lapped zippers

1 Thread a needle with doubled sewing thread in a color that matches the zipper (a contrast color is used here for clarity). At the required length, make five or six firm, straight stitches over the zipper teeth. Secure the thread with a couple of backstitches in the zipper tape.

2 Using pinking shears, cut off the zipper about ⅜" (1cm) below the stitches.

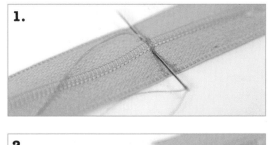

Automatic buttonhole

This function is not found on all machines, but is one that I recommend. It makes professional-looking buttonholes quickly and easily. Different sewing machines may have slightly different ways of making automatic buttonholes, so read your manual before trying one.

Check out...
Buying your first sewing
    machine, page 13
Stitches, page 23
How to run a sewing machine,
    page 21
Pressing, pages 26-27

Best used for...
Buttonholes in fabric

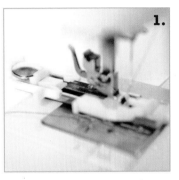

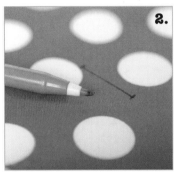

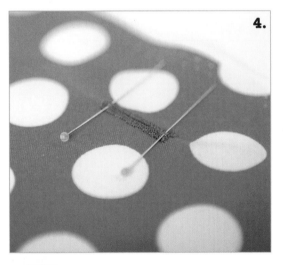

1 Fit the button you want to use into the buttonhole foot. The machine will automatically make a buttonhole the right size.

2 Mark the position of the buttonhole on the fabric.

3 Position the fabric under the foot so that the needle will start sewing at the end of the buttonhole nearest to you. Set the machine to the buttonhole function. Gently press the power pedal and the machine will sew the buttonhole. You need to be prepared to do some gentle steering, particularly when making buttonholes near seams, as lumps or ridges in the fabric can throw the buttonhole off

course. When the buttonhole is complete, pull the threads through to the back and trim them off.

4 Press the stitching. Put a pin in at each end of the buttonhole, just inside the end bars. These will make sure that you don't cut the threads by accident.

5 Using small, sharp-pointed scissors, very carefully cut the buttonhole open. Push one point of the scissors into the fabric in the middle of the buttonhole to start cutting to one end, then turn around and cut to the other end.

Manual buttonhole

If you don't have an automatic buttonhole function on your machine, then you can make them manually, but do practice first as they are tricky to get right. On some machines the zigzag is not as tight stitched in reverse as it is stitched forward, so the two sides of the buttonhole won't match perfectly.

Check out...
Stitches, page 23
How to run a sewing machine, page 21
Pressing, pages 26–27
Automatic buttonhole, page 58

Best used for...
Buttonholes in fabric

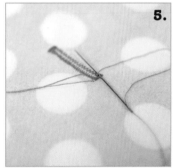

1 Mark the position of the buttonhole on the fabric. Set the sewing machine to a wide zigzag with zero stitch length. Position the fabric under the foot so that the needle will start sewing at the end of the buttonhole nearest to you. Make four or five stitches, ending with the needle on the left-hand side, but not down in the fabric.

2 Set the machine to a very narrow, tight zigzag. Press the reverse lever and slowly sew backward along the length of the marked line. The right-hand edge of the stitching should just cover the line. End with the needle on the left-hand side, but not down in the fabric.

3 Reset the sewing machine to a wide zigzag with zero stitch length. Make four or five stitches, ending with the needle on the right-hand side, but not down in the fabric.

4 Reset the sewing machine to a very narrow, tight zigzag. Sew forward until you reach the bar stitched in Step 1. The left-hand edge of the stitching should be very close to the stitches made in Step 2.

5 Pull all the threads through to the back. Thread them into a hand-sewing needle and weave them in and out of a few of the buttonhole stitches to secure them. Follow Steps 4–5 of Automatic Buttonhole to cut open the buttonhole.

Right: two automatic buttonholes (above), one with a button, and two manual buttonholes (below), one with a button.

In-seam buttonhole

This is essentially a gap in a seam through which you put a button and it is ridiculously simple to make. The pieces of thin fabric for the stays need to have the same laundering requirements as the main fabric.

Check out...

Stitches, page 23

How to run a sewing machine, page 21

Pinning, page 24

Pressing, pages 26-27

Sewing straight lines, page 30

Starting and finishing sewing, page 31

Finishing edges, page 32

Open seam, page 34

Best used for...

Buttonholes in seams

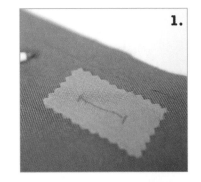

Above: two in-seam buttonholes, one with a button.

1 Using pinking shears, cut two pieces of very thin fabric (I have used organza—organdie or cotton lawn would also work), each 1¼" (3cm) wide by the required length of the buttonhole plus ¾" (2cm): these are the stays. Mark the length of the buttonhole centrally on one stay. On the main fabric, mark the seamline along the section where the buttonhole will be.

2 Lay the marked stay on the seamline where the buttonhole will be. Lay the other stay on the other side of the seam, matching the edges of them as best you can (they don't need to be perfectly aligned). Pin the stays in place, putting the pins in as you would if you were going to sew over them (which you aren't).

3 Set the sewing machine to a medium straight stitch and sew the seam up to the first pin. Reverse a few stitches to secure the seam. Turn the fabric around and sew the rest of the seam from the other end up to the other pin, reversing as before.

4 Press the seam open, then finish the edges of the seam allowances.

Ties

This technique can be used to make straps of any width and length to serve as bag handles, belts, dress straps, and curtain tab tops, as well as ties.

Check out...

Stitches, page 23

How to run a sewing machine,
    page 21

Pinning, page 24

Pressing, pages 26-27

Sewing straight lines, page 30

Starting and finishing sewing,
    page 31

Outward square corner, page 67

Best used for...

Straps of any width and length

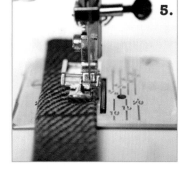

1 Cut on the straight grain a strip of fabric measuring four times the required width of the tie by the length plus ¾" (2cm). At each short end, press under ⅜" (1cm). Using small, sharp scissors, cut off the corners of the pressed-under section, as shown.

2 Wrong sides together, fold the tie in half along its length and press the fold.

3 Open the tie out flat. Fold one raw edge to the middle and press the fold along the length of the tie.

4 Fold in and press the other raw edge. Fold the whole tie in half along the line pressed in Step 2 and press it thoroughly.

5 Set the sewing machine to a medium straight stitch and fit the zipper foot. At one end of the tie, position the fabric with the edge of the foot against the open edge of the tie, so that the needle will start sewing close to the edge. You can check that it is positioned correctly by turning the handwheel to lower the needle until it just touches the fabric. Topstitch along the edge, reversing at each end to secure the stitching. If the ends of the tie are going to be hidden in a seam, then there is no need to sew across them. If they are going to be on display, then start at the fold edge on one short end, sew across to very close to the open edge, put the needle down into the fabric and pivot the tie around it before topstitching the open edge. Repeat to topstitch the other short end of the tie.

Right: a tie.

Rouleaux loops

These pretty fastenings are often used on wedding dresses and evening gowns, though they work well on any project requiring a feminine touch. Each loop must be long enough for the button to pass through plus 1¼" (3cm), so experiment before cutting the loop lengths. The loops are sewn into a seam between the main fabric and a facing and it's usually best to use iron-on interfacing to stiffen the facing.

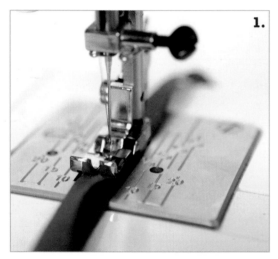
1.

2.

3.

4.

5.

Check out...

Stitches, page 23

How to run a sewing machine, page 21

Pinning, page 24

Basting, page 25

Pressing, pages 26–27

Sewing straight lines, page 30

Starting and finishing sewing, page 31

Finishing edges, page 32

Open seam, page 34

Making bias strip and binding, pages 74–75

Best used for...

Delicate fastenings

Lightweight and mediumweight fabrics

1 Cut a ¾"- (2cm-) wide piece of bias fabric long enough to make the required number of loops. Right sides together, fold it in half along its length. Set the sewing machine to a medium straight stitch and fit a ¼" (5mm) patchwork foot. At one end of the strip, position the fabric with the edge of the foot against the open edge of the strip and sew the seam. Cut the threads leaving 6" (15cm) tails.

2 Thread a blunt-tipped darning needle with one of the tails of thread. Slide the needle up the tube of fabric, working it along until it appears at the other end.

3 Pull the thread through, coaxing the end of the fabric it's attached to turn in and emerge at the other end of the tube. Keep pulling gently (you really don't want the thread to snap) to turn the whole tube right side out.

4 Cut off pieces of tube the required length. Fold them in half and press them flat so that the folded ends look like this.

5 Pin each loop in position on the right side of the fabric, matching the ends of the loop with the raw edge of the fabric. Baste the loops in place.

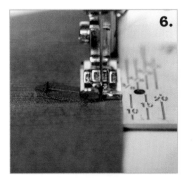

6.

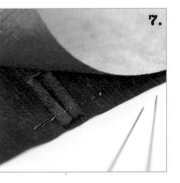

7.

8.

9.

10.

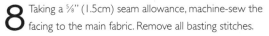

11.

10 Position the fabric under the needle with the presser foot on the seam allowances and the edge of it against the seamline of stitching. Understitch the facing by sewing the seam allowances to it.

11 Wrong sides together, fold the fabric and facing along the seam so that the loops protrude. Press the folded seam.

6 Fit a straight presser foot. Position the fabric under the needle with the edge of the presser foot against the raw edge of the fabric and machine-sew over the ends of each loop. Make sure that the loops remain at right angles to the raw edge of the fabric.

7 Right sides together, lay the facing on the main fabric, matching the raw edges. Pin the layers together and baste them if necessary.

8 Taking a ⅝" (1.5cm) seam allowance, machine-sew the facing to the main fabric. Remove all basting stitches.

9 Press both the seam allowances toward the facing.

> ### Sewing the bias strip
>
> If you don't have a ¼" (5mm) patchwork foot, cut the strip just a little wider and seam it using an ordinary straight presser foot. The principle is that the stitching should run more or less up the middle of the folded strip.

Right: rouleaux loops, two with buttons and two without.

Around the corner

Turning corners and sewing smooth curves are useful skills for all sorts of projects, from shirts to sheets. Done well, these techniques will lend a professional finish to your sewing, and they aren't difficult to master.

Inward square corner

The place you'll see this corner most often is on a square neckline where the facing is sewn to the main fabric. The corner needs to be really flat and smooth for the neckline to lie properly. The same principle can also be used to sew more tightly or widely angled corners.

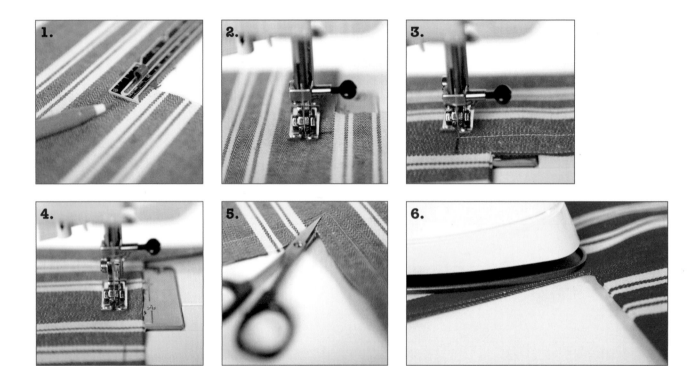

Check out...

Stitches, page 23

How to run a sewing machine, page 21

Pinning, page 24

Pressing, pages 26-27

Sewing straight lines, page 30

Starting and finishing sewing, page 31

Best used for...

Lightweight and mediumweight fabrics

1 On the first side you will sew, mark the end of the seam, ⅝" (1.5cm) beyond the corner. Pin the layers of fabric together.

2 Set the sewing machine to a medium straight stitch. Machine-sew the first side of the corner, stopping at the marked line with the needle down in the fabric.

3 Lift the presser foot and pivot the fabric around the needle until it is in the right position to sew the second side.

4 Machine-sew the second side of the corner.

5 Carefully snip into the seam allowances at the corner. Use the points of small scissors to snip down to about ⅛" (3mm) from the stitching.

6 Turn the corner right side out. Gently ease it into shape and press it thoroughly.

Left: an inward square corner.

Outward square corner

The corners of pillows and bags use this technique. Again, the same principle can also be used to sew more tightly or widely angled corners, though sharp points require a different treatment (see page 70).

1.

2.

3.

4.

Check out...

Stitches, page 23

How to run a sewing machine, page 21

Pinning, page 24

Pressing, pages 26–27

Sewing straight lines, page 30

Starting and finishing sewing, page 31

Inward square corner, page 66

Best used for...

Lightweight and mediumweight fabrics

1 On the first side you will sew, mark the end of the seam, ⅝" (1.5cm) up from the edge. Pin the layers of fabric together.

2 Set the sewing machine to a medium straight stitch. Machine-sew the first seam, then lift the presser foot and pivot the fabric as for Step 3 of Inward Square Corner. Machine-sew the second side of the corner.

3 Cut off the seam allowance on one side of the corner. Start about 2" (5cm) from the corner and cut at an angle to within about ⅛" (3mm) of the stitching.

4 Cut off the seam allowance on the other side of the corner in the same way. Turn the corner right side out. Gently ease it into shape and press it thoroughly.

Turning out corners

When you're turning the fabric right side out, do resist the temptation to use a knitting needle to push out the corner. It's all too easy to push the needle through the fabric or distort the corner beyond saving. Instead, use the end of a ruler, ideally a wooden or plastic one.

Right: an outward square corner.

Inward curve

Curved seams appear in many projects and it's worth learning how to treat the different curves to make them look their best. Inward curves require the seam allowances to be clipped so that they can stretch out to lie flat inside the curve.

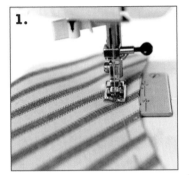

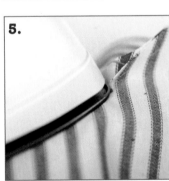

Check out...

Stitches, page 23

How to run a sewing machine,
    page 21

Pinning, page 24

Pressing, pages 26–27

Sewing straight lines, page 30

Starting and finishing sewing,
    page 31

Open seam, page 34

Best used for...

All fabrics

1 Pin the layers of fabric together. Set the sewing machine to a medium straight stitch and machine-sew the seam, taking a ⅝" (1.5cm) seam allowance.

2 Trim the seam allowances to about half their original width.

3 Cutting at an angle, snip into one seam allowance, snipping down to about ⅛" (3mm) from the stitching. Make these snips all the way along the curve, spacing them evenly about ¾" (2cm) apart.

4 Snip into the other seam allowance in the same way. Make the snips at the same angle and space them as before, but stagger them so that they lie between the snips in the first seam allowance.

5 Lay the seam over a tailor's ham and press the seam allowances open. Then turn the fabric right side out along the seam and press the seam flat.

Left: an inward curve.

Outward curve

With this curve the seam allowances need to squash up, so notches need to be cut to let them do this without making lumps in the fabric.

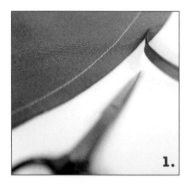

1.

2.

3.

4.

5.

1 Follow Steps 1–2 of Inward Curve to sew the seam and trim the seam allowances.

2 Cutting at an angle, snip into one seam allowance, snipping down to about ⅛" (3mm) from the stitching.

3 Cutting from the other direction, snip down to the tip of the first cut to cut out a tiny triangle of fabric. Make notches in this way right along the curve, spacing them about ¾" (2cm) apart.

4 Notch the other seam allowance in the same way, but stagger the notches so that they lie between those in the first seam allowance.

5 Turn the fabric right side out along the seam and ease and press it with your fingers to make the seam lie along the edge of the curve. Then press the seam flat.

Right: an outward curve.

Check out...

Stitches, page 23
How to run a sewing machine, page 21
Pinning, page 24
Pressing, pages 26–27
Sewing straight lines, page 30
Starting and finishing sewing, page 31
Open seam, page 34
Inward curve, page 68

Best used for...

All fabrics

Tight curves

For a tight curve, you may not be able to turn the fabric enough under the presser foot. With the needle down, lift the foot at regular intervals and pivot the fabric a little, similar to a square corner.

Scallops

These are a combination of inward corners and outward curves and so require a combination of the techniques to make them perfect.

Check out...

Stitches, page 23

How to run a sewing machine, page 21

Pinning, page 24

Pressing, pages 26–27

Starting and finishing sewing, page 31

Inward square corner, page 66

Outward curve, page 69

Best used for...

Lightweight and mediumweight fabrics

Above: a scalloped edge.

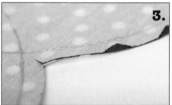

1 Pin together two pieces of fabric. Draw the scallops onto one of them; this pattern was made by drawing around a plate, overlapping each curve. Set the sewing machine to a medium straight stitch and machine-sew along the line. Lift the foot and pivot the fabric at the inward corners.

2 Cut out the scallops, cutting ⅜" (1cm) outside the stitching.

3 Snip into the inward corners. Notch the outward curves. Turn the scallops right side out along the seam and ease them into shape with your fingers. Press the seam.

Points

These are tightly angled outward corners, but they do need a slightly different treatment to make them lie neatly.

Above: a point.

Check out...

Stitches, page 23

How to run a sewing machine, page 21

Pinning, page 24

Pressing, pages 26–27

Starting and finishing sewing, page 31

Outward square corner, page 67

Best used for...

Lightweight and mediumweight fabrics

1 Follow Step 1 of Outward Square Corner to mark the end of the seam, then sew the first side. Lift the foot and pivot the fabric to make one stitch across the tip of the point. Pivot the fabric again to sew the second side of the point.

2 Trim the seam allowances as shown. Cut off the tip of the point ⅛" (3mm) from the stitching, then cut each side at an angle, following Steps 3–4 of Outward Square Corner.

Darts

These are little, angled pleats that shape fabric so that it lies smoothly around our curves. Well-sewn darts will make a good deal of difference to the fit of a garment.

Check out...

Stitches, page 23

Fabrics, page 22

How to run a sewing machine, page 21

Pinning, page 24

Basting, page 25

Pressing, pages 26–27

Sewing straight lines, page 30

Starting and finishing sewing, page 31

Best used for...

All fabrics

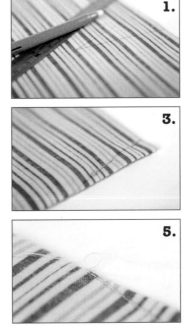

1.

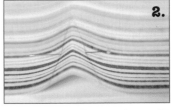

2.

3.

4.

5.

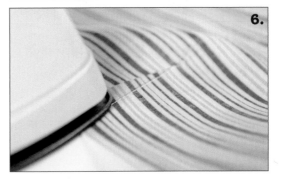

6.

1 Draw the dart on the wrong side of the fabric. If you are taking it from a pattern, make a tiny hole in the tissue at the tip of the dart then press the fabric marker over the hole to mark the tip on the fabric. Mark the top points of the dart and use a ruler to join the dots and so draw the dart.

2 Push a pin into the line on one side of the dart and push it out on the other line, making sure the pin is straight.

3 Push the layers of fabric together along the pin, then pin along the line with the head of the pin facing toward the point of the dart. If the fabric is slippery or otherwise tricky to sew, then baste just outside the marked line.

4 Set the sewing machine to a medium straight stitch. Starting at the edge of the fabric, machine-sew the dart. As you get to the tip, angle the stitching slightly so that the last couple of stitches run almost parallel to the fold.

5 Pull both threads through to one side and knot them firmly to secure the stitching. Remove any basting stitches.

6 Press the dart flat and then press it to one side. If it's a waist dart then press it toward the side seam, if it's a bust dart then press it downward. If the dart is very wide or the fabric very thick, cut away some of the fabric within the dart, leaving ⅜" (1cm) seam allowances.

Below: a dart.

On the edge

Bindings and trims have both practical and pretty aspects that make them great solutions to all sorts of sewing situations. Bind an edge to reduce bulk and add a pretty finishing detail at the same time, or slip a trim into a seam for a couture touch.

Making bias strip and binding

You can buy ready-made bias binding, but it's available only in limited colors. If you make your own—which is easy to do—then you can match or contrast it with your project to produce binding that adds an aesthetic as well as practical touch. You'll need a bias binding maker, which can be bought inexpensively at a sewing store. There are various ways of producing the initial parallelogram; this way is fabric-hungry, but it has the fewest number of seams and so is my preferred technique.

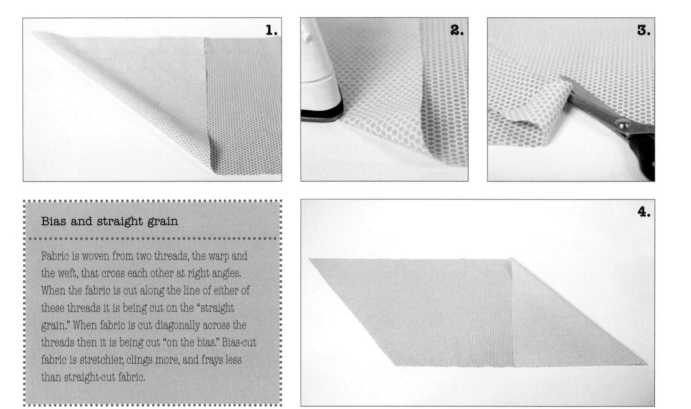

Bias and straight grain

Fabric is woven from two threads, the warp and the weft, that cross each other at right angles. When the fabric is cut along the line of either of these threads it is being cut on the "straight grain." When fabric is cut diagonally across the threads then it is being cut "on the bias." Bias-cut fabric is stretchier, clings more, and frays less than straight-cut fabric.

Check out...

Stitches, page 23
How to run a sewing machine, page 21
Pinning, page 24
Pressing, pages 26–27
Sewing straight lines, page 30
Starting and finishing sewing, page 31
Open seam, page 34

Best used for...

Lightweight and mediumweight fabrics
Woven fabrics

Making bias strip

1 Cut a rectangle of fabric on the straight grain and lay it flat and right side up. Fold one short end up to match the upper long edge. A triangle of the wrong side of the fabric is visible, as shown.

2 Press the diagonal fold.

3 Open the fabric out flat again and cut along the pressed fold to cut off the triangle of fabric.

4 Repeat Steps 1–3 to fold over, press, and cut off a triangle at the other end of the rectangle, folding it so that the pressed line will slope in the same direction as the first line to produce a parallelogram. The sloping ends are on the bias.

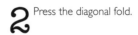

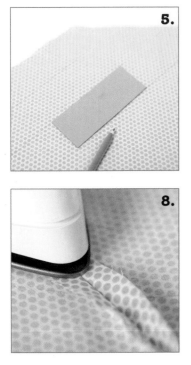

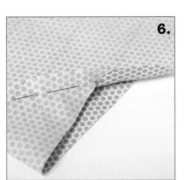

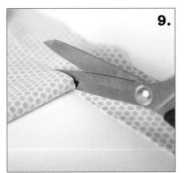

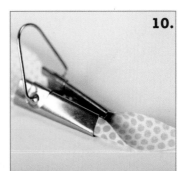

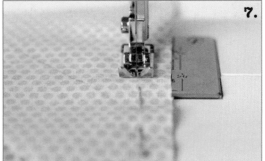

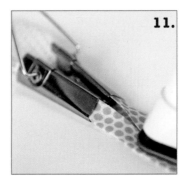

5 Cut a template strip of card that is the width of the fabric needed to make the bias binding. The packaging of your binding maker should tell you what width to use. On the back of the fabric, lay the template against one sloping edge of the fabric and draw along the other side of it, drawing a line that runs from one straight edge to the other straight edge, parallel to the slope. Then lay the template against this drawn line and draw a second line in the same way. Continue drawing lines across the fabric until you reach the other sloping edge, cutting off any excess along the last drawn line.

6 Right sides together, bring the two straight edges together. At one sloping end, match the bias edge with the first drawn line, thus offsetting all the lines by one. Make sure that the drawn lines match along the seam line, ⅝" (1.5cm) from the raw edges. Pin the straight edges together along the seam line to form a tube.

7 Set the sewing machine to a medium straight stitch and machine-sew the pinned seam, taking a ⅝" (1.5cm) seam allowance.

8 Press the seam open. You have made a tube of fabric with one continuous drawn line spiralling around it.

9 Starting at one end, cut along the drawn line to produce a continuous strip of bias tape.

Making bias binding

10 Feed one pointed end of the bias strip into the binding maker and pull it through.

11 Slowly pull the binding maker backward along the strip, pressing the folds flat as they emerge.

Right: handmade bias binding.

Decorative bias binding

To make the most of your handmade bias binding, apply it so that it's visible. Binding edges in this way means that there is no folded hem, so it's great for stiff or bulky fabrics. Binding is also a good finish for sheers as it avoids hemming issues and adds a little weight that can help the fabric hang better.

Check out...

Stitches, page 23

How to run a sewing machine, page 21

Pinning, page 24

Basting, page 25

Pressing, pages 26–27

Sewing straight lines, page 30

Starting and finishing sewing, page 31

Best used for...

Straight and curved edges

Make from lightweight and mediumweight fabrics

Trimming all fabrics

1 Open out one folded edge of the binding. Right sides together, pin the binding to the fabric, matching the raw edges.

Left: decorative bias binding on the right side of the project (above) and on the wrong side (below).

2 Baste the binding in place, stitching to one side of the fold (see Avoiding Pinholes, opposite).

3 Set the sewing machine to a medium straight stitch. Position the fabric in the sewing machine so that the needle will start sewing precisely on the opened-out fold in the binding. You can check that it is positioned correctly by turning the handwheel to lower the needle until it just touches the fabric. Machine-sew along the fold, reversing at each end to secure the stitching.

4 Remove the basting stitches and press the machine stitching flat. Fold the binding over the stitching so that it lies right side up and covers the raw edge of the fabric. Press the binding flat.

5 Fold the binding right over the raw edge of the fabric and to the wrong side. The free edge of the binding should just cover the line of stitching that shows on the wrong side (see inset). On the right side, pin the binding in place.

6 Position the fabric in the sewing machine so that the needle will start sewing precisely along the seam between the binding and the main fabric: this is called "stitch in-the-ditch." Machine-sew the binding in place, reversing at each end.

Hidden bias binding

With this method of binding an edge the binding itself is not visible, though the final line of stitching is. It's good for heavyweight fabrics, as you are avoiding a double fold, but not great for sheers because it tends to look odd. You can either make your own binding or, as it's not going to be seen, use a purchased bias binding, as here.

Check out...

Stitches, page 23
How to run a sewing machine, page 21
Pinning, page 24
Basting, page 25
Pressing, pages 26–27
Sewing straight lines, page 30
Starting and finishing sewing, page 31
Decorative bias binding, page 76

Best used for...

Straight and curved edges
Make from lightweight and mediumweight fabrics
Trimming all fabrics except sheers

Avoiding pinholes

If the fabric and binding don't mark when a pin is put in and taken out again, pin and baste the binding in place along the center. If holes do show, pin and baste along the folded-out edge of the binding, as opposite.

1 Follow Steps 1–4 of Decorative Bias Binding to sew one side of the binding in place and press it over the edge of the fabric.

2 Fold the full width of the binding to the wrong side of the fabric, folding over a little of the fabric as well. The amount of fabric folded over can be as much or as little as required: here, enough was folded over to make the gingham pattern look neat on the right side. On the wrong side, pin the binding in place.

3 Press the folded edge of the fabric, avoiding pressing the pins.

4 Position the fabric in the sewing machine so that the needle will start sewing close to the free edge of the binding. Machine-sew the binding in place, reversing at each end to secure the stitching.

Right: hidden bias binding on the right side of the project (above) and on the wrong side (below).

Zigzag bias binding

This is a quick and easy binding technique, but it's not good-looking and so best reserved for neatening edges that won't be seen, but that need to be well-finished. There is no need for a folded hem, so this is a good technique for bulky fabrics.

Check out...

Stitches, page 23

How to run a sewing machine,
    page 21

Pinning, page 24

Basting, page 25

Pressing, pages 26–27

Sewing straight lines, page 30

Starting and finishing sewing,
    page 31

Finishing edges, page 32

Best used for...

Straight and curved edges

Hidden edges

Make from lightweight and
    mediumweight fabrics

Trimming all fabrics

Left: zigzag bias binding looks the same on both sides.

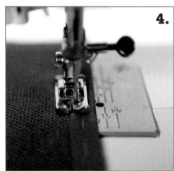

1 Fold the bias binding precisely in half and press it.

2 Slip the folded binding over the raw edge of the fabric, completely enclosing it. Pin the binding in place.

3 As it's a narrow edging, it's a good idea to baste the binding in place, especially if the fabric is slippery.

4 Set the sewing machine to a medium zigzag stitch. You can sew the binding in place in one of two ways, depending on the look you prefer and method you find easiest.

Turn the handwheel until the needle is as far to the right as it will go.

Position the fabric in the sewing machine so that the needle will start sewing on the binding, close to the edge. When the needle moves across to the left it will come down into the fabric, so the line of zigzag stitching will cover the join between the binding and the fabric.

For the other method, set the machine up in the same way but position the fabric so that the needle comes down on the right close to the outer edge of the binding. When it comes down on the left it should be close to the edge overlapping the fabric, so the line of stitching lies entirely on the bias binding.

Remove the basting stitches.

Shaping bias binding

Bias binding can be used on edges ranging from perfectly straight to tightly curved. However, if you are going to sew it to a curved edge you'll get a better finish if you shape it a bit first. You don't have to match the curve in the binding precisely to the edge being bound, but the nearer you get, the better.

Check out...

Stitches, page 23

How to run a sewing machine, page 21

Pressing, pages 26–27

Sewing straight lines, page 30

Decorative bias binding, page 76

Hidden bias binding, page 77

Zigzag bias binding, page 78

Best used for...

Curved edges

Make from lightweight and mediumweight fabrics

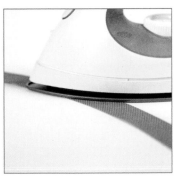

If the binding is going to enclose the edge, as for Decorative or Zigzag Bias Binding, fold the binding in half. For Hidden Bias Binding have it flat, as here. Press the iron down onto the binding close to one end, then pull the binding through under the iron, pulling it round to create a curve as you do so. How tightly round you pull the binding will dictate how tight the curve will be.

Right: bias binding shaped to a curve.

Straight binding

If the edge you are binding is straight, with no hint of a curve, then you can make the binding from fabric cut on the straight grain rather than on the bias. This is easier in that you just have to cut strips of fabric rather than create the bias parallelogram, but the techniques for applying it are exactly the same as for bias binding.

Check out...

Stitches, page 23

How to run a sewing machine, page 21

Pressing, pages 26–27

Sewing straight lines, page 30

Making bias strip and binding, pages 74–75

Decorative bias binding, page 76

Hidden bias binding, page 77

Zigzag bias binding, page 78

Best used for...

Straight edges

Make from lightweight and mediumweight fabrics

Trimming all fabrics

Right: a straight-bound edge using the Decorative Bias Binding technique.

Binding a corner

Using bias binding to trim neat, square corners is not difficult as long as you sew, measure, and fold accurately. It's a good way of trimming place mats made from heavyweight, heatproof fabric.

Check out...

Stitches, page 23

How to run a sewing machine,
 page 21

Pinning, page 24

Pressing, pages 26–27

Sewing straight lines, page 30

Starting and finishing sewing,
 page 31

Outward square corner, page 67

Making bias strip and binding,
 pages 74–75

Decorative bias binding, page 76

Best used for...

Square corners

Make from lightweight and
 mediumweight fabrics

Trimming all fabrics

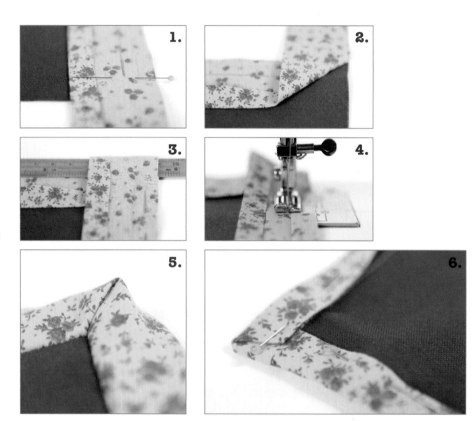

1 Follow Steps 1–2 of Decorative Bias Binding to baste the binding in place along one side of the corner. Measure back half the folded width of the binding from the corner and put in a pin to mark the spot. Position the fabric in the sewing machine so that the needle will start sewing precisely on the opened-out fold in the binding. Machine-sew along the fold as far as the pin, reversing at each end to secure the stitching.

2 Take out the pin and fold the binding straight up so that the fold lies diagonally across the corner.

3 Lay a ruler along the edge the binding is sewn to, matching it to the raw edges of the fabric and binding. Fold the binding straight down over the ruler so that the opened-out edge is matched to the raw edge of the fabric on the second side of the corner. Pin this edge in place.

4 Starting from the very top, at the folded-over edge, sew the binding to the fabric along the second side. Sew on the fold as before.

5 Turn the binding right side out over the corner of the fabric. It should turn easily and need minimal coaxing to form a perfect miter.

6 On the back, fold the binding over to cover the visible lines of stitching and arrange the corner as neatly as possible. Follow Step 6 of Decorative Bias Binding to finish the binding, pivoting the fabric around the needle at the corner.

Left: a bound corner.

Piping

Piping is set into a seam and is sometimes thought of as a rather old-fashioned technique, but that's only true if the project and fabric you use are dated. Use piping to emphasize an outline shape, in a vivid color to add an accent, or in patterned fabric to create detail in an otherwise plain project.

Check out...

Stitches, page 23

How to run a sewing machine, page 21

Pinning, page 24

Basting, page 25

Pressing, pages 26–27

Sewing straight lines, page 30

Starting and finishing sewing, page 31

Open seam, page 34

Making bias strip and binding, pages 74–75

Best used for...

Straight and curved edges and seams

Make from lightweight and mediumweight fabrics

Trimming all fabrics

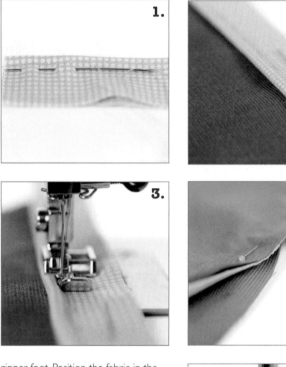

1 Make bias strip wide enough to encircle the piping cord plus 1¼" (3cm). Right side out, wrap the piping around the cord, matching the long raw edges and leaving a tail of cord protruding at each end. Baste the layers of fabric together, stitching close to, but not tight against, the cord. Note that this fabric has a diagonal check pattern, so when cut on the bias the pattern looks square.

2 Lay the piping on the right side of one piece of fabric, matching the raw edges. Pin the piping in place.

3 Set the sewing machine to a medium straight stitch and fit a zipper foot. Position the fabric in the sewing machine with the side of the foot tight against the cord. Machine-sew the piping in place, reversing at each end to secure the stitching.

4 Lay the piped piece of fabric on top of the other piece, matching the raw edges. Pin the layers together.

5 Machine-sew as in Step 3, crowding the foot as tightly against the cord as possible so that this second line of stitching is a tiny bit closer to the cord than the first line. (If the first line of stitching is visible, your piping won't look very professional.)

Right: piping can be set into an edge seam (above) or an open seam within a project (below).

In-seam trim

Setting fancy trims into a seam is a fabulous and easy way of adding decorative detail to a simple project. You need a trim fit for the purpose—with one flat, stable edge that can be sewn into the seam—and there are literally thousands to choose from.

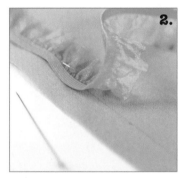

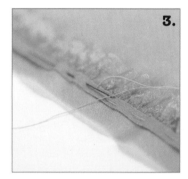

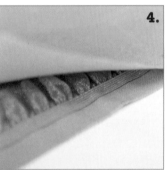

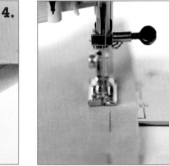

Check out...

Stitches, page 23

How to run a sewing machine, page 21

Pinning, page 24

Basting, page 25

Pressing, pages 26-27

Sewing straight lines, page 30

Starting and finishing sewing, page 31

Open seam, page 34

Best used for...

Straight and curved edges and seams

Trimming all fabrics

Left: a trim can be set into an edge seam (above) or an open seam within a project (below).

1 Using a fabric marker and a seam gauge to measure accurately, mark the ⅝" (1.5cm) seam allowance on one of the pieces of fabric.

2 Pin the trim to the right side of the fabric, with the flat edge just over the marked line toward the raw edge.

3 Baste the trim in place, stitching through the flat edge. After finishing the basting, fold the seam allowance to the wrong side to check that none of the flat part of the trim shows beyond the marked line.

4 Lay the other piece of fabric right side down on top of the trimmed piece, matching the raw edges. Pin the layers together.

5 Set the sewing machine to a medium straight stitch. Sew the seam, taking an accurate ⅝" (1.5cm) seam allowance.

6 If the trim is to protrude from an edge seam, fold the fabric along the seam and press the fold only very carefully to avoid crushing the trim.

Edge trims

As well as trims designed to be set into a seam, there are many, many other types and styles of trim that work well sewn to the edge of a project. Here are just a few examples with information on how best to sew them on.

Check out...

Stitches, page 23

How to run a sewing machine, page 21

Pinning, page 24

Basting, page 25

Pressing, pages 26–27

Sewing straight lines, page 30

Starting and finishing sewing, page 31

Best used for...

Straight and curved edges and seams

Trimming all fabrics

Choosing trims

There are some practical aspects to think about when choosing a trim for a project. The trim and fabric should have the same laundering requirements: a dry-clean only trim on a cotton dress isn't a good idea. Also, the trim can't be too heavy for the fabric or the project won't hang properly. A little weight can be good, but a chunky, beaded trim on a floaty fabric won't work.

Do think about how you are going to attach a trim before just machining it on across the middle. This trim already had a line of machine stitching attaching the ruffled section to the velvet ribbon, so another line on the opposite edge of the ribbon looked fine. However, insensitive machine sewing can spoil a trim and some may be best attached using tiny hand stitches.

Some trims that aren't designed to be sewn into a seam will, in fact, work well when used that way. This sample shows wide rickrack set into an edge seam, producing a delicate scallop.

The visible line of stitching needed to hold up a hem can detract from a pretty trim, but this isn't a problem on faced edges. This daisy trim is positioned half on, half off the fabric to add shaped detail to the edge. A line of stitching very close to the edge of the fabric holds the trim in place and understitches the facing at the same time, preventing it rolling forward.

An edge with a narrow hem can be detailed with flat braid that has at least one shaped edge that protrudes beyond the fabric. Sew it on with a line of machine stitching that holds the braid in place and the hem up at the same time. Do make a small test sample because a double hem topped by braid can be very chunky.

Fancy that

You, and your sewing machine, can produce gorgeous, decorative details that will add a glamorous touch to the most straightforward sewing projects. None of these techniques are difficult to master, though you will find that you have more choices to make than you do with purely practical techniques.

Gathered ruffle

An easy-to-make, feminine detail that looks great on women's and girl's garments alike. Made from crisp cotton they have a charming retro feel, while in filmy organza they are wonderfully romantic.

Above: a gathered ruffle that has been set into an edge seam.

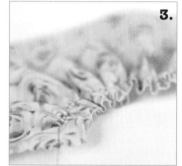

How much ruffle?

Before you make miles of ruffles for a project, make some samples to see how the fabric gathers up and to decide how much you'll need. Twice the desired length, as used here, produces a soft ruffle in cotton, but in fine, sheer fabric you will probably need at least three times the length to make a ruffle that has any body to it.

Check out...
Stitches, page 23
How to run a sewing machine,
     page 21
Sewing straight lines, page 30
Starting and finishing sewing,
     page 31
Double hem, page 43
Narrow hem, page 43

Best used for...
Lightweight and
     mediumweight fabrics

1 Cut a strip of fabric twice the desired length of the ruffle, by the depth plus 1" (2.5cm): this is enough to make the hem and set the ruffle into a seam at the top. Using either the Double Hem technique (for cotton fabric) or the Narrow Hem technique (for sheer or silky fabric), make a ¼" (5mm) double hem along one long edge, which will be the bottom of the ruffle. If the short ends are going to be visible, hem them, too.

2 Set the sewing machine to a long straight stitch and loosen the tension. Position the fabric right side up in the sewing machine with the edge of the presser foot against the top raw edge. Sew right along the top edge, without reversing at the beginning or end of the stitching.

3 Starting at one end, pull gently on the bobbin thread to start gathering the fabric. Keep pulling, easing the gathers along to the middle. When you have gathered about half the ruffle, knot the threads and start

gathering from the other end. Pull and ease the gathers along gently: if you break the thread you'll have to start again. Once the ruffle is gathered up to the required length, knot the second set of threads.

4 Set the sewing machine to a medium straight stitch and set the tension correctly for the fabric. Taking a ⅜" (1cm) seam allowance, sew along the top of the ruffle, sewing the gathers down to stop them shifting about. Sew slowly and use your fingers to keep the gathers feeding evenly under the needle rather than bunching up into clumps. Reverse at each end to secure the stitching.

Knife pleats

These are my favorite style of pleat as they are quick to make and look great almost anywhere. Put them into the seam along the edge of a pillow, add them to the top of a purse, or the bottom of a dress—anywhere they'll fit. The pleats are best made from fabric with a little body to it or they become floppy and the effect is lost.

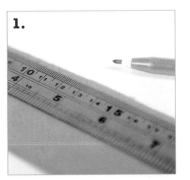
1.

2.

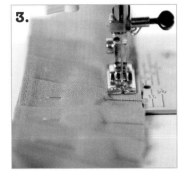
3.

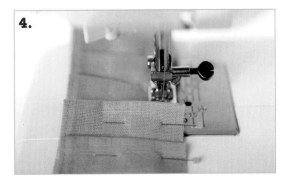
4.

Above: knife pleats that have been pressed and set into an edge seam.

Check out...

Stitches, page 23

How to run a sewing machine, page 21

Pinning, page 24

Sewing straight lines, page 30

Starting and finishing sewing, page 31

Double hem, page 43

Narrow hem, page 43

Gathered ruffle, page 86

Best used for...

Mediumweight fabrics

1 Follow Step 1 of Gathered Ruffle, but cut the strip of fabric three times the desired length. Along the top edge, measure and mark out the pleats on the right side of the fabric. They can be between ⅝" (1.5cm) and 1¼" (3cm) wide: any narrower and they resemble gathers and any wider and they loose their crispness. These pleats are ¾" (2cm) wide, so there are little marks that distance apart right along the top edge of the strip.

2 Right side up, pleat the fabric along the marked edge. Each pleat works over three marks: you pinch the fabric at the first mark, fold it over at the second mark, and then bring the first mark down to touch the third mark. Repeat with the next group of three marks. Put a vertical pin in each pleat as you make it, with the head of the pin against the top edge of the fabric.

3 Set the sewing machine to a medium straight stitch. Taking a ⅜" (1cm) seam allowance, sew across the tops of the pleats to hold them in place. Sew slowly, taking out the pins as you get to them rather than sewing over them. Reverse at each end to secure the stitching. You can press the finished pleats for a crisper effect or leave them soft, as you prefer.

4 Even with the pleats pinned, it's easy for the toe of the presser foot to just slip underneath the edge of a pleat and fold it over, as shown, so keep a careful eye on what's happening. If you're at all concerned, take the extra time and baste the pleats using small stitches.

Box pleats

These are slightly more complicated pleats to make, but they do look beautiful and are very versatile. You can make a narrow band of them, as here, to use as a trim, or you can add them into an existing garment pattern. You need to be quite confident in your sewing to do this.

Above: box pleats that have been pressed and set into an edge seam.

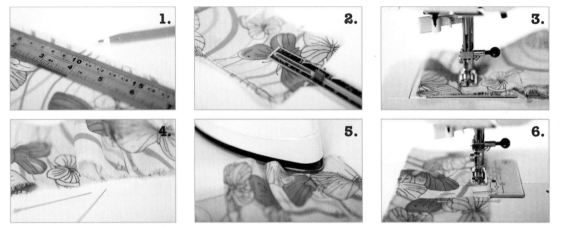

Check out...

Stitches, page 23

How to run a sewing machine, page 21

Pinning, page 24

Pressing, pages 26-27

Sewing straight lines, page 30

Starting and finishing sewing, page 31

Double hem, page 43

Narrow hem, page 43

Knife pleats, page 87

Best used for...

Mediumweight fabrics

1 Follow Step 1 of Knife Pleats to cut and hem the fabric. Box pleats can be almost any width; here they are 3" (8cm). For pleats this wide, measure and mark on the wrong side of the fabric ¾" (2cm) from one short end. Then make marks alternately 3" (8cm) and 1½" (4cm) apart, ending with a 3" (8cm) mark and a final ¾" (2cm) of fabric.

2 Wrong side up, pleat the fabric along the marked edge. These pleats work over two marks; simply match the first and second marks and put in a vertical pin, and repeat with every pair of marks. The pins will be sewing guides, so it's important that you put them in squarely. To check this, fold the fabric and put the head of the pin in where the two marks touch. Use a seam gauge to measure 1½" (4cm) from the fold and make sure the pin emerges at this measurement.

3 On the right side, starting about halfway down from the top edge, sew each pleat. This distance will vary depending on the effect you want. If you aren't sure, baste a few pleats first to see how they look. Position the fabric in the sewing machine at the required distance from the top edge with the needle in line with the tip of the pin. Reverse a few stitches, then take out the pin and sew in a straight line to the marks on the top edge of the strip. Reverse to secure the stitching.

4 Lay the strip of pleated fabric right side up, so the stitched folds are facing you. Pinch the top of each fold to make a tiny crease, then flatten the fold, matching the crease to the line of stitching underneath. Put in a vertical pin on each side of the line of stitching to hold the box pleat.

5 To make sure the pleats are even and square before you sew them in place, press the bottom edge of each one. Adjust the fabric, re-pinning if necessary, to make each pleat lie flat next to its neighbor.

6 Follow Step 3 of Knife Pleats to sew across the top edge of the box pleats.

Pintucks

This is a technique that can be used almost anywhere to create a lovely vintage look. Garments of all sorts, bags, pillows, scarves, bed linen…anything made from a fairly crisp, lightweight to mediumweight fabric can benefit from the addition of a few pretty pintucks. You can make pintucks in sheer and floaty fabrics, but it's not that easy and I would recommend basting before machine sewing.

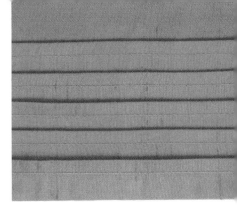

1.

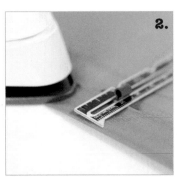
2.

3.

Above: pintucked silk fabric.

4.

5.

Check out...
Stitches, page 23
How to run a sewing machine, page 21
Pressing, pages 26–27
Sewing straight lines, page 30
Starting and finishing sewing, page 31

Best used for...
Lightweight and mediumweight fabrics
Fabrics with a crisp finish

1 Make and press a fold in the fabric ¾" (2cm) from the edge, making sure the fold is parallel to the edge.

2 Open the first fold out flat. Using a seam gauge to measure accurately, make and press another fold ¾" (2cm) from the first fold and parallel to it. Continue making folds in this way until a fold has been made for each pintuck required.

3 Set the sewing machine to a medium straight stitch. Starting with the last fold made, position the fabric in the sewing machine so that the needle will start sewing very close to the folded edge. You won't be able to use the marks on the throat plate to guide you, so choose another point on the machine bed to line up the edge of the fabric with: here, it is the inside edge of the right-hand fed dog. Machine-sew along the fold, reversing at each end to secure the stitching.

4 Move along to the next fold and repeat Step 3. Continue until each fold has been stitched and all the pintucks have been made.

5 Press all the pintucks flat, pressing them in whichever direction you prefer.

Sewing on ribbon or braid

Fabulous for dressing up a project or customizing a garment, these trims aren't difficult to sew on, but do practice sewing straight lines.

Above: sewn-on ribbon.

Check out...

Stitches, page 23

How to run a sewing machine, page 21

Pinning, page 24

Basting, page 25

Sewing straight lines, page 30

Starting and finishing sewing, page 31

Best used for...

All fabrics

1 Pin then baste the ribbon or braid to the fabric in the desired position. Baste a little way in from the edges.

2 Set the sewing machine to a medium straight stitch. Position the fabric in the sewing machine so that the needle will start sewing very close to the edge of the ribbon: the closer the better. You won't be able to use the marks on the throat plate to guide you, so you really need to concentrate on keeping the fabric running straight. The tricks are to sew slowly and to watch the position of the edge of the presser foot, not the needle because the up-and-down motion will distract you. Machine-sew along the ribbon, reversing at each end to secure the stitching.

3 Starting at the same end of the ribbon as for the first line of stitching, sew along the other edge in the same way. It's important to start at the same end each time as close rows of stitches running in opposite directions can distort the fabric and then the ribbon won't lie flat.

Sewing on rickrack

This is one of the cutest trims there is and it gives a great retro look to children's and adults' garments alike.

Check out...

Stitches, page 23

How to run a sewing machine, page 21

Pinning, page 24

Basting, page 25

Sewing straight lines, page 30

Starting and finishing sewing, page 31

Best used for...

All fabrics

Below: sewn-on rickrack.

1 Pin then baste the rickrack to the fabric. Baste along one edge, making a stitch through each scallop.

2 Set the sewing machine to a medium straight stitch. Position the fabric in the machine so that the needle will start sewing along the center of the rickrack. Check where one edge of the presser foot is in relation to the scalloped edge. Start to machine-sew very slowly, keeping the edge of the presser foot in the same

place in relation to the scallops. If you try to watch where the needle is going, the up-and-down motion combined with the zigzagging of the rickrack will have you sewing a wobbly line almost immediately.

Sewing on lace

Delicate and romantic, lace can be sewn on as an edging or it can be inserted into fabric using this technique. The gorgeous, very professional-looking, result is surprisingly easy to achieve. It's always worth making a test sample using the project lace and fabric to check that it looks as you hoped it would and that the lace works with the weight of the fabric. The technique is shown here with straight-edged lace, but it works equally well with a shaped edge.

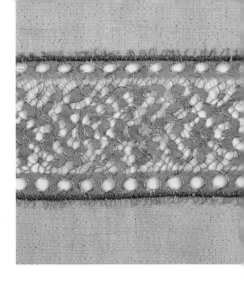

1.

2.

3.

Above: inset lace.

4.

5.

6.

Check out...

Stitches, page 23
How to run a sewing machine, page 21
Pinning, page 24
Basting, page 25
Sewing straight lines, page 30
Starting and finishing sewing, page 31
Sewing on ribbon or braid, page 90

Best used for...

Lightweight fabrics

1 Pin the lace in the desired position on the fabric.

2 Lay the fabric (and pinned-on lace) right side down. Using the backs of the pins as a guide, lay a strip of tear-away stabilizer, cut a little wider than the lace, over the back of the fabric where the lace is pinned on.

3 On the right side, baste through all the layers, stitching a little way in from the edges of the lace. Then take out all the pins.

4 Set the sewing machine to a narrow, tight zigzag stitch. Position the fabric in the machine so that the needle will start sewing close to the edge of the lace: the precise position will depend on the nature of the edge of the lace. This lace has a very delicate fringe, so the stitching lies just inside that. You can check that it is positioned correctly by turning the handwheel to lower the needle until it just touches the lace and then continuing to turn it to make one complete zigzag stitch. Follow Steps 2–3 of Sewing On Ribbon Or Braid to machine-sew the lace to the fabric.

5 Lay the fabric right side down and carefully tear way the stabilizer from the stitching. You may need to use tweezers to get all the shreds out of the back of the stitches without pulling them too hard.

6 Using small, sharp embroidery scissors, VERY CAREFULLY cut away the fabric between the lines of zigzag stitching. Cut as close to the stitches as possible without actually cutting into them.

Above: a free-motion embroidered flower.

Free-motion embroidery

The steps below offer a simple introduction to the wide, and exciting, world of embroidery using your sewing machine, a world I hope you'll want to explore further. Do read the appropriate section in your sewing machine manual as different machines have different ways of setting up for free-motion embroidery. You will certainly have to drop the feed dogs and either fit an embroidery (sometimes called darning) foot or take the foot off completely. If you do the latter then you must be very careful not to sew your fingers. Move the fabric under the needle by holding the outer edge of the hoop, not by pushing the fabric with your hands.

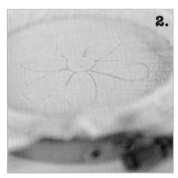

Check out...

How a sewing machine works, page 10

Stitches, page 23

How to run a sewing machine, page 21

Best used for...

All fabrics

1 Using a fabric marker, draw a motif onto the fabric.

2 Lay the fabric on a piece of tear-away stabilizer the same size and fit both layers into an embroidery hoop. Fit them in so that the inner hoop in on top of rather than underneath the fabric.

3 Set the sewing machine to straight stitch with a stitch length

of zero, drop the feed dogs, and fit an embroidery foot. Position the fabric in the machine with the needle to one side of the motif. Turn the handwheel to take the needle down and up again, pulling a loop of the bobbin thread to the right side. Hold both threads to one side as you start stitching. After a few stitches you can cut them off.

4 As the feed dogs are disengaged, it's the speed and direction in which you move the hoop that controls the length and direction of the stitches. Hold the hoop on either side and move it so that the needle will start sewing on the motif. Slowly press the power pedal to begin stitching and move the hoop so that the line of stitches follows the drawn line. You can go backward and forward to make the line thicker as desired.

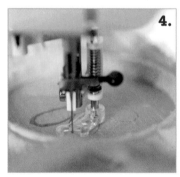

Binding the hoop

Binding the inner ring of the embroidery hoop with thin, bias-cut fabric (see Making Bias Strip And Binding, page 74) allows it to grip the embroidery fabric better, with less risk of marking or otherwise damaging it. Just wrap the fabric strip very tightly around the ring, securing the end on the inside with a few small stitches.

Appliqué

There are various types of appliqué and the style shown here is that most often used with a sewing machine. As with free-motion embroidery (opposite), there is a wide range of techniques to explore further.

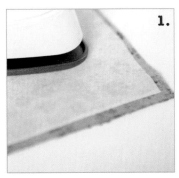

1.

2.

Check out...

Stitches, page 23

How to run a sewing machine,
    page 21

Best used for...

All fabrics

*Above; an appliquéd
heart motif.*

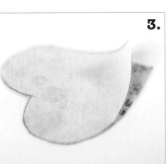

3.

4.

5.

1 Following the manufacturer's instructions, iron fusible webbing onto the back of a piece of fabric.

2 Using a pencil, draw the required motif onto the paper backing of the webbing. Remember that as you are drawing on the back, the shape will be reversed when seen from the right side: this matters if you are drawing, for example, letters or numbers.

3 Cut out the motif and peel off the backing paper.

4 Again following the manufacturer's instructions, iron the motif onto the right side of the background fabric.

5 Set the sewing machine to a wide, tight zigzag; this is known as satin stitch. Turn the handwheel until the needle moves across to the right. Position the fabric in the sewing machine so that when the needle comes down on the right-hand side of the stitch, it will pierce the fabric just outside the edge of the motif. Sewing slowly, satin stitch right around

the motif. If you need to pivot the fabric (for example, to turn a corner), stop sewing with the needle down in the fabric on the right-hand side of the stitch. Lift the presser foot and turn the fabric as needed, then continue stitching. In this way the stitched outline will remain smooth.

Patchwork

Machine-sewn patchwork is a huge subject, and there are many, many specialist books detailing different techniques and block patterns. Here is a flavor of what can be achieved by simply arranging squares and sewing seams. The more accurately you cut, sew, and match seams, the better the patchwork will look.

Above: a simple patchwork.

Check out...

Stitches, page 23

How to run a sewing machine, page 21

Pinning, page 24

Pressing, pages 26–27

Sewing straight lines, page 30

Starting and finishing sewing, page 31

Finishing edges, page 32

Open seam, page 34

Intersecting seams, page 39

Best used for...

Lightweight and mediumweight fabrics

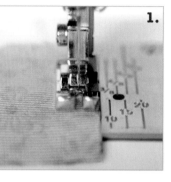

1 Cut squares of different fabrics the required size plus ¼" (5mm) all around. Set the sewing machine to a medium straight stitch. Right sides together and taking ¼" (5mm) seam allowances (a patchwork foot with a ¼" (5mm) toe is very useful here), pin then machine-sew squares together to make a strip the desired length. Repeat the process to make as many strips as needed.

2 Trim the ends of the seam allowances at an angle, as shown.

3 Press the seam open.

4 Right sides together, pin the strips together, carefully matching the seams.

5 Taking ¼" (5mm) seam allowances, machine-sew the strips together to make a patchwork.

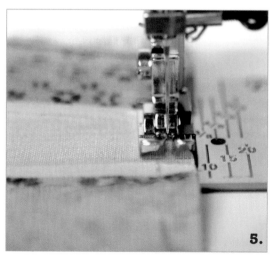

Quilting

As with patchwork, quilting on the sewing machine offers a wide range of possibilities and we have only the space to explore the basic principles here. But they are great principles and you can easily take them further. Remember to always test stitch tension on a sample made up of scraps of all the fabrics.

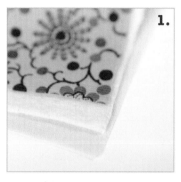

Above: simple quilted fabric.

Check out...

Stitches, page 23

How to run a sewing machine,
    page 21

Pinning, page 24

Basting, page 25

Sewing straight lines, page 30

Starting and finishing sewing,
    page 31

Best used for...

Lightweight and
    mediumweight fabrics

1 You need a main fabric, batting, and backing, the latter two being up to 2" (5cm) larger than the main fabric. A wool batting is used here. Layer the fabrics with the lining right side down, then the batting (matching the raw edges), then the main fabric right side up and centered. Pin the layers together around the edges.

2 Starting at one corner, baste diagonally across to the opposite corner. Repeat in the other direction to form an X shape. Then baste a cross, working from the midpoint of one edge straight across to the midpoint of the opposite edge, and the same in the opposite direction. Take out pins as they become redundant. Finally, baste around the edges. This basting may seem time-consuming, but it will stop the layers shifting around as you machine-sew and it is worth doing. However, if the project is very small (perhaps less than 8" (20cm) square), then a diagonal cross and the edge basting may be enough.

3 To quilt a simple pattern of lines, start at the midpoint of one edge. Set the sewing machine to a medium straight stitch and thread it with machine quilting thread if required, though you can use a normal sewing thread. If you have a walking foot for quilting, then fit it, otherwise use a straight presser foot. Machine-sew straight across the fabric, reversing just a few stitches at each end.

4 A quilting bar fits onto the presser foot and the width can be set as required. Position the fabric in the sewing machine so that the end of the bar sits on the first line of stitching. Machine-sew across the fabric, keeping the end of the bar running along the stitches. Continue in this way, machining a few lines across the fabric in one direction. Then turn the bar around and machine the same number of lines in the other direction. Continue in this way until the fabric is completely quilted.

Make me, make me!

Now that you can sew, what do you want to make? Your newly acquired skills and a little practice will let you create gorgeous garments, desirable accessories, fabulous soft furnishings, and anything else you might want to sew. Here are some specially designed, easy-to-make projects to get you started in the wonderful world of sewing.

Zipped up

With its flattering flared shape and fashionable handkerchief hemline, this simple-to-make skirt suits—and will fit—all shapes and sizes. If you make the skirt length longer than mid-calf at the back, then the points of the hem may trail on the floor at the front, but other than that there are no specific dos and don'ts. The waist ease allows the top of the skirt to sit on the hips, which works best with the shape, and it can either lie with the V at the front, as shown, or on one hip. You can use any fabric you want, though heavyweight fabrics may not drape very well.

You will need...

1 piece of fabric measuring the desired skirt length at center back plus 2¾" (7cm), by the circumference of your waist plus ¾" (2cm) ease plus twice the desired skirt length plus 2¾" (7cm). (For example, you want the skirt to be 25½" (65cm) at center back so the fabric length will be 25½" (65cm) + 2¾" (7cm) = 28¼" (72cm). Your waist measures 28" (71cm), so the fabric width will be 28" (71cm) + ¾" (2cm) + 25½" (65cm) + 25½" (65cm) + 2¾" (7cm) = 82½" (210cm). You can join fabric using an open seam at center back to get a piece the right width.)

Iron
Ironing board
Pins
Scissors
Seam gauge
Tape measure
Sewing machine
Sewing thread to match fabric
Hand-sewing needle
Basting thread
A zipper that is 2½" (6cm) shorter than the desired skirt length
Hook and loop fastening

Check out...

Stitches, page 23
How to run a sewing machine, page 21
Pinning, page 24
Basting, page 25
Pressing, pages 26–27
Sewing straight lines, page 30
Starting and finishing sewing, page 31
Open seam, page 34
Double hem, page 43
Corner hem, pages 46–47
Centered zipper, pages 52–53
Shortening a zipper, page 57

Choosing a zipper

Standard dress zippers come in the widest range of colors, but if you can find a separating zipper in the right color you can use that instead. In that case, choose a zipper that is 1½" (4cm) shorter than the skirt length. Don't machine-sew a section of the seam, just fit the zipper using the Separating Zipper method (see page 55). With some fabrics, such as denim, a metal zipper can look cool.

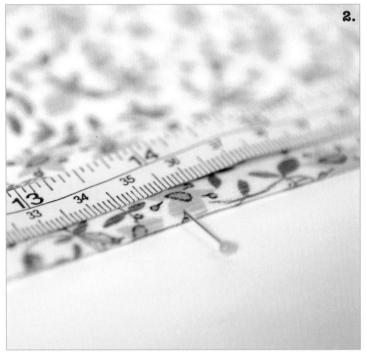

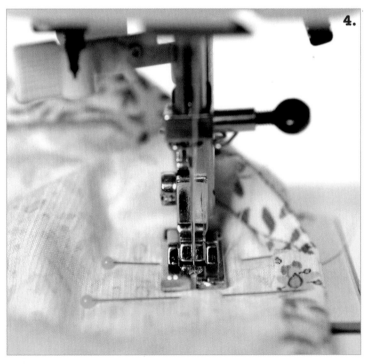

1 Turn under, press, and pin a double hem around all four edges of the fabric. Miter each corner, following Steps 1–8 of Corner Hem, but do not machine sew the hem at this stage.

2 Fold the fabric in half across its length and put in a pin on the fold: this is center back. Measure half your waist circumference plus ⅜" (1cm) out to each side from the fold and put in pins: these mark the start of the zipper. Drape the fabric around your waist, pinning it together at the start of the zipper, and check that the waist is comfortable and that the skirt is the desired length.

3 Right sides facing, fold the fabric in half again. On the waist edge, open out the pressed hem above the mitered corner and pin the layers together along the second pressed fold of the double hem, pinning as far as the pins marking the start of the zipper.

4 Put in horizontal pins 1½" (4cm) and 2¼" (6cm) from the corner. Set the sewing machine to a medium straight stitch. Machine-sew along the pressed fold between the pins, reversing at each end to secure the stitching.

5 Baste along the pressed fold from the end of the machine-sewn section to the pins marking the start of the zipper.

6 Position the zipper with the pull just below the marking pins: the end stop should be just within the machine-sewn section. Pin, baste, and machine-sew the zipper in place. Remove all basting stitches.

7 Hand-sew the hook and loop fastening to the zipper tape, just above the pull.

8 Machine-sew the double hem right around the fabric, pivoting neatly at the corners.

Sleep on it

Pillowcases are so easy to make and provide the perfect way of jazzing up a plain bed linen set. Make them in good-quality cotton (the kind sold for quilting is perfect) if you are going to actually sleep on them, and in any fabric you like if they are going to be purely decorative. You can also make a matching bed banner for a great finishing accent. This one is quilted with irregularly spaced lines for a contemporary, asymmetric look that complements the fabric pattern.

You will need...

For the pillowcase:

A piece of fabric measuring twice the length of your pillow plus 8" (20cm), by the width plus 1¼" (3cm)

Sewing thread to match the fabric

For the banner:

2 pieces of main fabric each measuring the width of your bed plus 16" (40cm), by the desired depth of the banner plus 1¼" (3cm) (You can join fabric using open seams to get pieces the right width.)

1 piece each of backing fabric and polyester batting measuring 2" (5cm) larger all around than the main fabric

Basting thread

Hand-sewing needle

Quilting thread darker than the main fabric

Sewing thread to match the main fabric

For both:

Seam gauge

Tape measure

Iron

Ironing board

Pins

Sewing machine

Scissors

Check out...

Stitches, page 23

How to run a sewing machine, page 21

Pinning, page 24

Basting, page 25

Pressing, pages 26–27

Sewing straight lines, page 30

Starting and finishing sewing, page 31

Finishing edges, page 32

Open seam, page 34

Double hem, page 43

Quilting, page 95

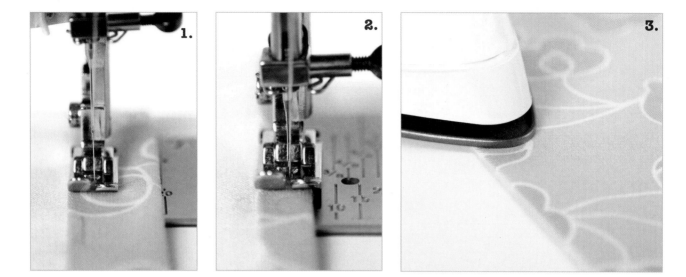

Pillowcase

1 Set the sewing machine to a medium straight stitch and at one short end of the piece of fabric, make a double hem.

2 At the other end make a narrower double hem, turning under ⅜" (1cm) for each fold.

3 Measure the length of your pillow from the end with the standard double hem made in Step 1. Wrong sides together and raw edges matching, press a fold across the fabric at this measured length.

4 Turn the fabric right sides together and fold it at the pressed line, matching the raw edges again. Approximately 5½" (14cm) will extend beyond the double hem: fold this piece right side down over the double hem.

5 Pin the raw edges together; these are the side seams. Taking a ⅝" (1.5cm) seam allowance, machine sew the side seams. Zigzag the seam allowances together. Turn the pillowcase right side out and press it.

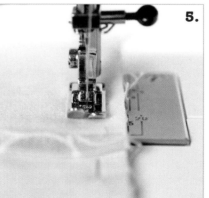

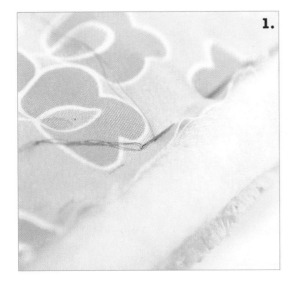

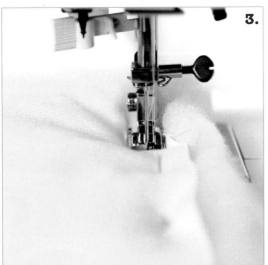

Banner

1 Assemble the layers—the backing fabric right side down, the batting, and one piece of main fabric right side up. Baste a diagonal and a straight cross through all the layers, then baste around the edges.

2 Set the sewing machine to a medium straight stitch and thread it with the quilting thread. Roll up the banner as tightly as possible so that the roll will pass through the sewing machine to the right of the needle. Quilt a series of irregularly spaced vertical lines across the banner, sewing from one long edge straight across to the other one. If you have joined fabric then make sure that quilting lines run along the seam lines to hide them—this is called "stitch in-the-ditch." Remove the basting stitches.

3 Right sides together, lay the second piece of main fabric over the quilted piece. Pin the layers together around the edges. Machine-sew around the edges taking a ⅝" (1.5cm) seam allowance and leaving a 6" (15cm) gap close to the end of one long edge. Zigzag the seam allowances together then trim off any excess batting.

4 Turn the banner right side out through the gap. Press the edges and slipstitch the gap closed.

The classy cook

Be the complete domestic goddess with an apron that's so pretty you'll want to keep it on even when you're not in the kitchen. It's easy to make and doesn't need much fabric, so sew one to match every party outfit and be the most stylish cook in town. This version is trimmed with rickrack, but you should choose a trim to complement your fabric.

You will need...

1 piece of main fabric measuring half your waist measurement plus 10" (26cm), by the desired length of the apron plus 2¼" (6cm)
Fabric marker
Compasses or dinner plate
Scissors
Seam gauge
Iron
Ironing board
Pins
Enough medium rickrack to go around the hemmed edges of the apron and around your waist plus 2" (5cm)
Hand-sewing needle
Basting thread
Sewing machine
Sewing threads to match fabrics and rickracks
2 pieces of contrast fabric and 1 piece of mediumweight iron-on interfacing each measuring your waist measurement plus 4" (10cm), by 3½" (9cm)
Enough wide rickrack to go around your waist plus 2" (5cm)
Template on page 127
1⅛" (28mm) self-cover button
Scrap of main fabric

Check out...

Stitches, page 23
How to run a sewing machine, page 21
Cutting out, page 25
Pinning, page 24
Basting, page 25
Pressing, pages 26–27
Sewing straight lines, page 30
Starting and finishing sewing, page 31
Double hem, page 43
Outward curve, page 69
Curved hem, page 45
Automatic buttonhole, page 58
Box pleats, page 88
Sewing on rickrack, page 90

Choosing fabric

If your apron is going to be as practical as it is pretty, then you must choose fabrics and trim that can with stand the hot wash that may be needed to remove food stains. Quilting cotton is a good choice as it's got enough body to make a crisp apron.

1. Round off the two lower corners of the main fabric: you can do this using compasses, or by drawing around the edge of a dinner plate, then cut off the excess fabric. Turn under and pin a double ⅝" (1.5cm) hem down each side, around the curved corners, and along the bottom edge.

2. Pin then baste the medium rickrack around the turned-under edges. Set the sewing machine to a medium straight stitch and machine sew the rickrack in place, sewing the hem at the same time. Remove the basting stitches.

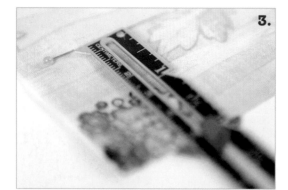

3.

4.

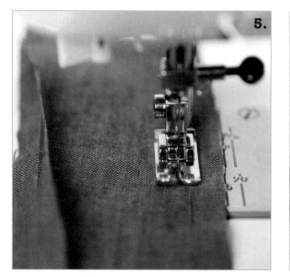

5.

6.

3 In the raw top edge of the fabric, make two equally spaced box pleats. Each pleat uses 4" (10cm) of fabric and is positioned about 4" (10cm) in from a hemmed edge. Stitch 2" (5cm) down each pleat then open them out and baste across the top of them.

4 Iron the interfacing onto the back of one piece of the contrast fabric; this will be the inside of the waistband. Enlarge the template by 150% and cut it out to make a pattern. Fold the contrast fabric in half lengthways and pin the pattern to it with the short straight edge against the fold. Cut out the shape, extending it past the jagged lines to the edge of the fabric. Cut the same pattern out of the second piece of contrast fabric.

5 Press under ⅜" (1cm) along the long straight edge on both pieces of contrast fabric. Open the fold out flat again. Right sides together, pin the pieces to each other. Taking a ⅝" (1.5cm) seam allowance, machine-sew along the short sides and the top curved edge.

6 Turn the waistband right side out. Press the seam and re-press the fold along the long straight edge.

7 Make a buttonhole in one end of the waistband, positioning it horizontally and centrally.

7.

8.

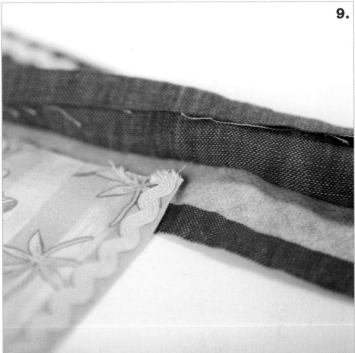

9.

10.

11.

12.

8 Pin, baste, and machine-sew the remaining medium rickrack along the top edge of the waistband. Fold it over at each end to neaten it.

9 Put in pins to mark the center of the waistband and the center of the apron section. Lay the waistband right side up and flat. Matching the pins, slip ⅝" (1.5cm) of the top of the apron between the pressed-under edges of the waistband. Pin the pressed edges of the waistband together right along their length, pinning the apron section in place as you go.

10 Machine sew along the waistband, close to the pressed edges. Remove all basting stitches.

11 Pin then baste the wide rickrack over the stitching along the edge of the waistband. At the front, where the apron joins the waistband, shift the rickrack down slightly to cover the join between the fabrics. Machine-sew the rickrack in place, folding it over at each end to neaten it. Remove the basting stitches.

12 Following the manufacturer's instructions, cover the button with the scrap of main fabric. Sew the button to the waistband to align with the buttonhole in the other end.

Shop til you drop

This eco-friendly, good-looking, and easy-to-sew tote can be made in any sturdy fabric and to whatever size you need, just change the measurements as required. The enclosed and bound seams are strong and they keep the inside of the bag neat, so no fraying strands will entangle themselves around your purchases. Pick fabric to go with your coat for seriously coordinated grocery shopping.

You will need...

2 pieces of main fabric each
    measuring 14 x 15¼" (35 x 38cm)
Sewing machine
Sewing threads to match fabrics
Seam gauge
Iron
Ironing board
Pins
14" (35cm) of 1" (2.5cm) bias binding
Tape measure
2 pieces of main fabric each
    measuring 4¾ x 14" (12 x 35cm)
1 piece of contrast cotton measuring
    26¾ x 2¾" (67 x 7cm)
Scissors
Hand-sewing needle
Basting thread

Check out...

Stitches, page 23
How to run a sewing machine,
    page 21
Pinning, page 24
Basting, page 25
Pressing, pages 26–27
Sewing straight lines, page 30
Starting and finishing sewing,
    page 31
Open seam, page 34
Mock French seam, page 35
Faced hem, page 49
Ties, page 61
Zigzag bias binding, page 78

1 Set the sewing machine to a medium straight stitch. Right sides together and using a mock French seam, sew the two large pieces of main fabric together along the long sides. Press the seams flat.

2 Making sure the side seams are at the sides and taking a ⅝" (1.5cm) seam allowance, sew across one short end of the fabric tube.

3 Press under ⅝" (1.5cm) at each end of the bias binding and press it in half along its length. Pin the binding across the seamed short end, over the seam allowance, and zigzag it in place.

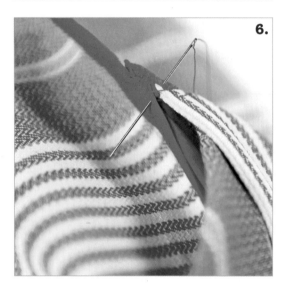

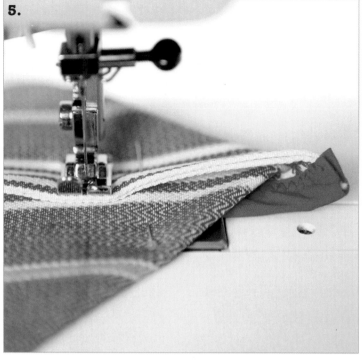

4 Flatten out one corner of the bag, arranging it so that the side seam and base seam align on opposite sides of the point. Press the corner flat and pin it.

5 Measure 2¾" (7cm) along the side seam from the point and draw a line across the corner at right angles to the seam. Machine sew along the drawn line, reversing at each end to secure the stitching. Sew the other bottom corner in the same way.

6 Hand-sew the points of the corners to the bound seam along the bottom of the bag.

7 Make a tie from each of the small pieces of main fabric, but do not turn under the short ends. These will be the bag handles.

8 Turn the bag right side out and lay it flat. Pin one end of a handle to the front of the bag, 3" (8cm) from the left-hand side seam and with the seam facing to the right. Match the end of the handle with the raw edge of the top of the bag.

Choosing fabric

I've used a traditional ticking fabric to make my shopping tote. Cotton duck, denim, or canvas would also work well. If you are worried that the handles won't be strong enough to cope with all your purchases, slide a length of grosgrain ribbon between the folds before sewing the edges.

9 With the seam facing to the left (and making sure the handle isn't twisted), pin the other end to the front of the bag, 3'' (8cm) from the right-hand side seam. Pin the other handle to the other side of the bag in the same way. Machine-sew back and forth over each end of each handle a few times, stitching the ⅜'' (1cm) from the edge. At this stage the handles will look as though they are sewn on upside down.

10 Join the short ends of the contrast strip using an open seam and zigzag the seam allowances. Press under ⅝'' (1.5cm) along one edge.

11 Right sides together, matching the raw edges and matching the open seam to a bag side seam, pin the contrast strip to the top of the bag.

12 Machine-sew the contrast strip to the top of the bag taking a ⅝'' (1.5cm) seam allowance. Trim and zigzag the seam allowances and understitch them as for a faced hem. Turn the contrast strip to the inside and press the top edge. The bag handles are now the right way up. Flatten the contrast strip against the inside of the bag and pin then machine-sew around the bottom edge.

Wrapped in ruffles

Shown here as an elegant evening accessory made in dupioni silk, this versatile, simply designed wrap can have a very different feel in another fabric. Make it in lightweight woolen fabric as a glamorous extra layer in winter, or in pretty cotton for a vintage-style cover-up to go with a summer dress.

You will need...

1 piece of fabric measuring 6¼ x 140" (16 x 350cm) (this can be made by joining several smaller pieces using open seams)

Sewing machine

Sewing thread to match fabric

Seam gauge

Iron

Ironing board

Tape measure

2 pieces of fabric each measuring 16 x 56" (40 x 140cm)

Compasses or dinner plate

Fabric marker

Scissors

Pins

Basting thread

Hand-sewing needle

Check out...

Stitches, page 23

How to run a sewing machine, page 21

Pinning, page 24

Basting, page 25

Pressing, pages 26–27

Sewing straight lines, page 30

Starting and finishing sewing, page 31

Finishing edges, page 32

Open seam, page 34

Outward curve, page 69

In-seam trim, page 82

Gathered ruffle, page 86

Two-color wrap

You can choose different color fabrics for the two sides of your wrap. Remember that the ruffle will show on both sides in the same color, so your choices do need to work well with each other. You can also choose different types of fabric, as long as they can be laundered together.

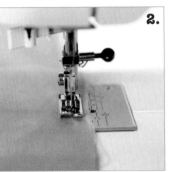

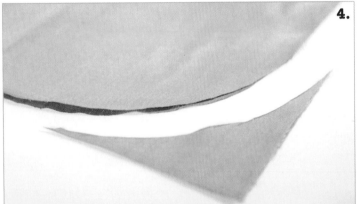

1. Set the sewing machine to a medium straight stitch. On each short end of the long strip of fabric, make a ⅜'' (1cm) double hem.

2. Set the sewing machine to a long straight stitch and loosen the tension. Fold the strip of fabric in half along its length, matching the two raw edges. Treating it as one layer of fabric, sew a line of gathering stitches along the edge. Don't forget to re-adjust the tension as soon as you finish the gathering.

3. Pull up the gathers until the strip measures approximately 80'' (200cm) long.

4. Lay the large pieces of fabric on top of one another. Round off the two lower corners using compasses, or by drawing around the edge of a dinner plate, then cut off the excess fabric. Press under ⅜'' (1cm) along the top straight edge.

5. Right side up, lay one of the large pieces of fabric flat. Starting at one pressed top edge and matching the raw edges, pin the ruffle to the fabric.

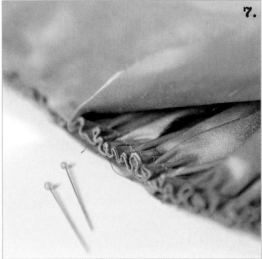

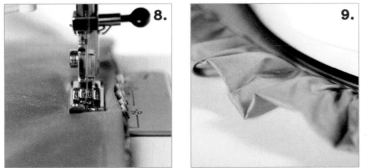

6 Pin the ruffle around the curved edge of the fabric, finishing at the other end of the pressed top edge. Adjust the gathers to fit if needed. Baste the ruffle in place.

7 Right side down, lay the other large piece of fabric on top of the ruffled piece. Pin the pieces together around the ruffled edge.

8 Set the sewing machine to a medium straight stitch. Machine sew the layers together, taking a ⅝" (1.5cm) seam allowance. Remove the basting stitches, clip the curves, then zigzag the seam allowances together.

9 Turn the wrap right side out and carefully press the seam, being sure not to press and crush the gathers.

10 Match the pressed top edges and pin them together. Machine sew them, sewing very close to the edge.

Tied up

Pillows are great projects for novice sewers—easy and quick to make, decorative to look at, and not very fabric hungry. The steps are shown here are for a pillow with ribbon ties, but the same principles apply for the button and rouleaux loop variations.

You will need...

1 piece of fabric measuring 12 x 39"
   (30 x 100cm)
4 lengths of ⅝" (1.5cm) grosgrain
   ribbon, each measuring 20" (50cm)
Tape measure
Pins
Seam gauge
Basting thread
Hand-sewing needle
Sewing machine
Sewing thread to match fabric
Scissors
Iron
Ironing board
Cushion pad measuring 12 x 18"
   (30 x 45cm)

Check out...

Stitches, page 23
How to run a sewing machine,
   page 21
Pinning, page 24
Basting, page 25
Pressing, pages 26–27
Sewing straight lines, page 30
Starting and finishing sewing,
   page 31
Finishing edges, page 32
Open seam, page 34
Double hem, page 43
Automatic buttonhole, page 58
Rouleaux loops, pages 62–63

VARIATIONS

A button-fastened pillow is made in the same way as a tie-fastened one, but make one hem deep enough to easily accommodate the buttonholes (you'll need to alter the length measurement of the fabric accordingly). Make the buttonholes, then fold the buttonhole end over first. Make up the cover and sew on buttons to match the buttonholes.

For a rouleaux fastening, you'll need to cut a facing piece of fabric. Make the loops and position them on one short end of the cover fabric. Sew the facing on, fold it to the back, and press the seam. This end of the cover is folded over first. Make up the cover and sew on buttons to match the loops.

1 At one short end of the fabric, lay a piece of ribbon on the right side, 4" (10cm) in from and parallel to the edge. Match one raw end of the ribbon to the raw edge of the fabric. Position another length of ribbon in the same way, but placing it 4" (10cm) from the other edge. Pin the ribbons in place.

2 Fold a ⅜" (1cm) double hem, folding the ends of the ribbons into the hem as you do so. Baste the hem, making sure that the ribbons stay at right angles to the edge.

3 Set the sewing machine to a medium straight stitch. Machine-sew the hem close to the inner folded edge, then sew it again, close to the outer folded edge.

4 At the other short end of the fabric, machine-sew a ⅜" (1cm) double hem. Measure down 3" (8cm) from the hem. Pin the end of a piece of ribbon to the fabric at this point, positioning it 4" (10cm) in from and parallel to the raw edge. Position the final length of ribbon in the same way, but placing it 4" (10cm) from the other edge.

5 Set the sewing machine to a very narrow, tight zigzag stitch. Stitch across the end of a piece of ribbon, down one side for ⅜'' (1cm), across the ribbon, and then up the other side to the starting point. Sew on the other length of ribbon in the same way.

6 Roll up each ribbon and pin it to keep it out of the way. Right side up, lay the fabric flat. Measure 6¼'' (16cm) from the end with the ribbons sewn into the hem and fold the fabric at this point.

7 Measure 12'' (30cm) from the other end and fold the fabric at this point. This end will overlap the first folded end.

8 Pin the raw edges together. Machine-sew the seams taking ⅝'' (1.5cm) seam allowances then zigzag the seam allowances together.

9 Turn the pillow cover right side out and press it. Insert the pad and tie the ribbons into bows. Trim the ends of the ribbons at an angle.

Put on the cuffs

Make this really pretty ribboned cuff in a colorway to go with your favorite party outfit: in fact, if you have sewn the outfit then use the same fabric for your cuff for the ultimate in coordinated jewelry. You only need little scraps of trim, so raid your stash and add buttons and beads to your cuff if you wish.

You will need...

2 pieces of fabric and a piece of iron-on mediumweight interfacing each measuring the circumference of your wrist plus ¾" (2cm), by 3" (8cm)

Scissors

Tape measure

Iron

Ironing board

Scraps of ribbons and rickrack, each at least 3" (8cm) long

Seam gauge

Pins

Hand-sewing needle

Basting thread

Sewing machine

Sewing thread to match fabric and ribbons

4 small eyelets

Eyelet setting kit

1 piece of organza ribbon measuring 8" (20cm) long

Check out...

Stitches, page 23

How to run a sewing machine, page 21

Pinning, page 24

Basting, page 25

Pressing, pages 26-27

Sewing straight lines, page 30

Starting and finishing sewing, page 31

Finishing edges, page 32

Open seam, page 34

Sewing on ribbon or braid, page 90

Sewing on rickrack, page 90

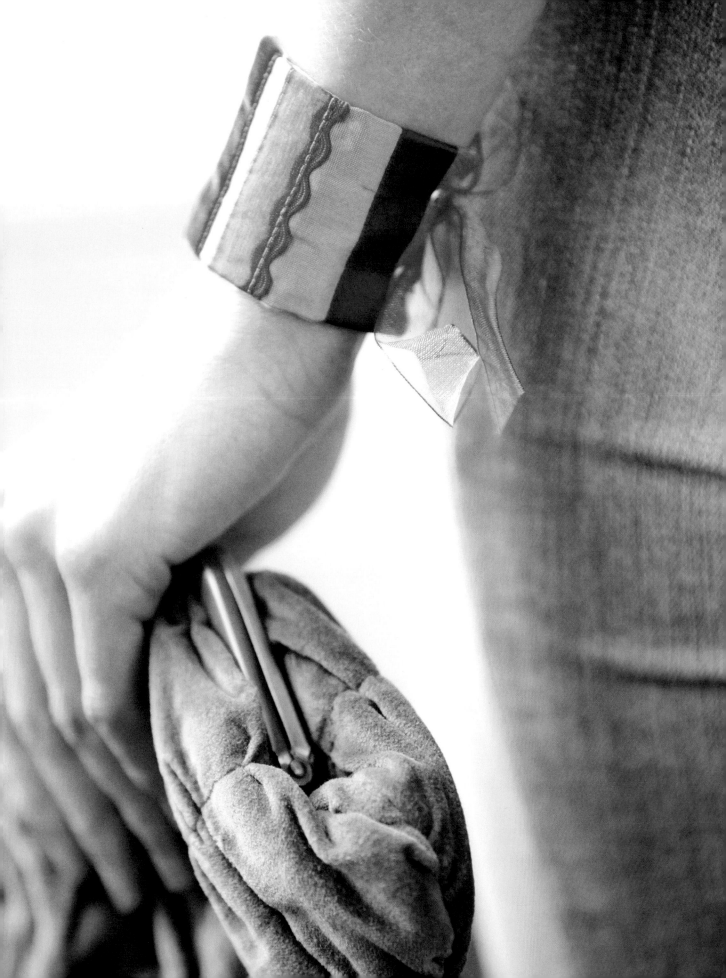

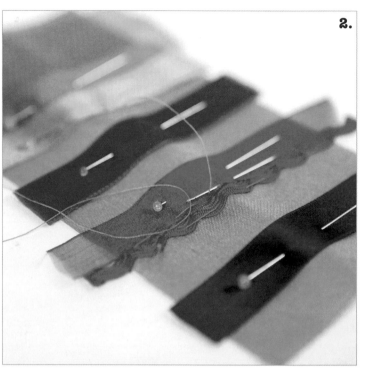

1 Iron the piece of interfacing onto the back of one of the pieces of fabric; this will be the right side of the cuff.

2 Arrange the ribbons and rickrack on the interfaced fabric, keeping them 1" (2.5cm) from the short ends. When you are happy with the arrangement, pin and then baste all the ribbons in place. If you want to overlap pieces of ribbon, as here, you will need to baste and machine-sew the lower layers before basting the top layers.

3 Machine-sew each length of ribbon to the fabric. Remove the basting stitches.

4 With right sides facing, lay the other piece of fabric on top of the beribboned piece, matching the raw edges. Pin the layers together.

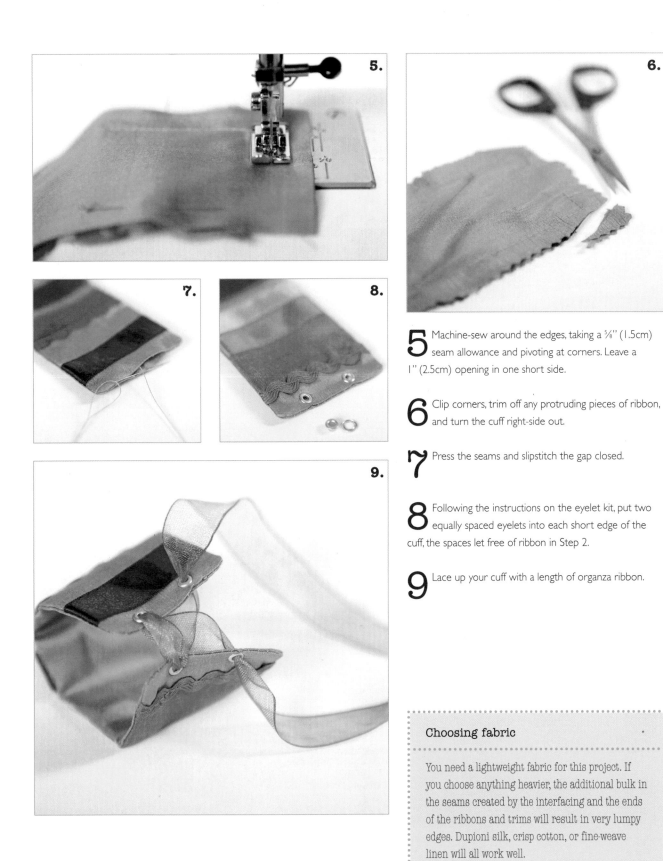

5.

6.

7.

8.

9.

5 Machine-sew around the edges, taking a ⅝'' (1.5cm) seam allowance and pivoting at corners. Leave a 1'' (2.5cm) opening in one short side.

6 Clip corners, trim off any protruding pieces of ribbon, and turn the cuff right-side out.

7 Press the seams and slipstitch the gap closed.

8 Following the instructions on the eyelet kit, put two equally spaced eyelets into each short edge of the cuff, the spaces let free of ribbon in Step 2.

9 Lace up your cuff with a length of organza ribbon.

Choosing fabric

You need a lightweight fabric for this project. If you choose anything heavier, the additional bulk in the seams created by the interfacing and the ends of the ribbons and trims will result in very lumpy edges. Dupioni silk, crisp cotton, or fine-weave linen will all work well.

Glossary

I've made this book as jargon-free as possible, but there might be some terms that mystify you. Here is a list of the most commonly used and an explanation of what they really mean.

Appliqué A decorative technique where a shape is cut from one fabric and sewn onto another (see Appliqué, page 93).

Basting Sewing layers of fabric together to hold them temporarily until the final sewing is complete (see Basting, page 25).

Bias strip A strip of fabric that is cut at 45° to the straight grain. Such strips can be folded and made into bias binding (see Making Bias Strip and Binding, pages 74–75).

Clip To make small cuts into the seam allowance with the points of scissors (see Outward Curve, page 69).

Dart A stitched fold of fabric used to shape a garment (see Darts, page 71).

Facing A piece of fabric that is sewn to the main piece then turned to the back so that the seam allowances are hidden (see Rouleaux Loops, pages 62–63).

Feed dogs These are the "teeth" that lie under the throat plate of the sewing machine and feed the fabric through it (see How A Sewing Machine Works, page 11).

Finishing edges Sewing or binding raw edges of fabric to stop them fraying (see Finishing Edges, page 32).

Fusible webbing This is heat-activated fabric glue that comes in a very thin sheet on a paper backing (see Appliqué, page 93).

Gathering Sewing a line of stitches along the edge of a piece of fabric, then pulling them tight to ruffle up the fabric (see Gathered Ruffle, page 86).

Hem allowance The amount of fabric that is folded over to make a hem. If more than one fold is made, then the hem allowance is the total amount of fabric needed to make all the folds (see Hem Allowance, page 42).

Interfacing A woven or knitted fabric that is used to support and stiffen areas of garments and other sewing projects. Fusible interfacing has one side with heat-activated glue and it can be ironed onto fabric (see Rouleaux Loops, pages 62–63).

Miter An angled join at a square corner (see Corner Hem, pages 46–47).

Notch To cut small V-shapes into the seam allowance with the points of scissors (see Inward Curve, page 68).

Pivot To put the sewing machine needle down into the fabric, lift the presser foot, and turn the fabric around the needle so you can start sewing in a new direction (see Inward Square Corner, page 66, and Outward Square Corner, page 67).

Presser foot The part of the sewing machine that holds the fabric flat against the feed dogs while it is being sewn. There are different presser feet for various sewing tasks (see Sewing Machine Accessories, pages 14–15).

Raw edge A cut edge of fabric that has not been finished by sewing or binding (see Finishing edges, page 32).

Right side This is the side of the fabric that will be facing outward on the finished project. It is sometimes abbreviated to RS.

Rouleaux A thin tube of bias fabric that is folded and sewn into a seam to make a loop (see Rouleaux Loops, pages 62–63).

Seam allowance The amount of fabric between the raw, cut edge and the line of stitching that makes the seam. In dressmaking the standard seam allowance is ⅝" (1.5cm), though you should always check a sewing pattern to see what it requires (see Sewing Straight Lines, page 30).

Selvage The edge along the length of the fabric that is created during production and won't fray (see Single Hem, page 42).

Sheer fabric Fabric that is translucent.

Stabilizer A product that is laid on the back of fabric to support it while it is being worked on. Once the work is complete, the stabilizer is removed. There are various different types suitable for different tasks and fabrics (see Sewing On Lace, page 91, and Free-motion Embroidery, page 92).

Straight grain The directions that the threads that make up the fabric run in. The warp runs lengthwise and the weft runs widthwise. When the fabric is cut along the line of either of these threads it is being cut on the "straight grain." When it is cut on the weft this is sometimes called being cut on the "cross grain."

Understitch To sew a line of stitches within the seam allowance to hold a facing flat (see Rouleaux Loops, pages 62–63).

Wrong side This is the side of the fabric that will be facing inward on the finished project. It is sometimes abbreviated to WS.

Template

The Classy Cook, pages 106–109
Waistband template, enlarge by 150%

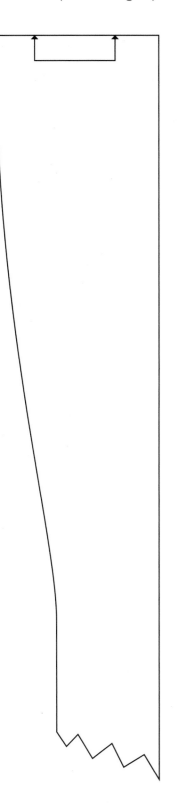

Resources

LIBERTY OF LONDON
Great Marlborough Street
London W1B 5AH
Tel: 011 44 20 7734 1234
www.liberty.co.uk
Supplier of Liberty fabrics.

REPRODEPOT FABRICS
www.reprodepot.com
Supplier of vintage fabrics.

SEW, MAMA, SEW!
www.sewmamasew.com
Supplier of cotton fabrics,
magazines, and trims.

JANOME
www.janome.com
The brand of sewing machine
and accessories that I use.

SUPERBUZZY
www.superbuzzy.com
Supplier of imported fabrics,
notions, magazines, and trims.

MOOD FABRICS
225 West 37th Street, 3rd Floor
New York, NY 10018
Tel: 212 730 1030
www.moodfabrics.com
Supplier of garment and
upholstery-weight fabrics, as well
as notions and trims.

FABRITOPIA
www.fabritopia.com
Supplier of a selection of
popular designer fabrics.

THE COTTON PATCH
www.quiltsusa.com
Supplier of a wide selection of
fabrics and sewing machines.

Acknowledgments

My thanks to Paula Breslich for commissioning this book and to Katie
Hardwicke for ensuring that it made sense. Dominic Harris took the
gorgeous step and style photographs and Louise Leffler was the brilliant
book designer. Laura Wheatly and Camilla Coburn Davis were the
glamorous models. And thanks, as always, to Philip for putting up with it all.

Index

Appliqué 93
Around the corner 64–71
Automatic buttonhole 58

Basting 25
Bias binding
    binding a corner 80
    decorative bias binding 76
    hidden bias binding 77
    making bias strip and binding 74–75
    shaping bias binding 79
    zigzag bias binding 78
Binding a corner 80
Blind-stitch hem 44
Box pleats 88
Buttonholes
    automatic buttonhole 58
    in-seam buttonhole 60
    manual buttonhole 59
Buying your first sewing machine 13

Centered zipper 52–53
Classy cook, The 106–109
Corner hem 46–47
Corners
    inward square corner 66
    outward square corner 67
Curved hem 45
Curves
    inward curve 68
    outward curve 69
Cutting out 25

Darts 71
Decorative bias binding 76
Double hem 43

Edge trims 83

Fabrics, threads, and stitches 22
Faced hem 49
Fancy that 84–95
Fastened up 50–63
Finishing edges 32
Flat fell seam 38
Free-motion embroidery 92
French seam 36

Gathered ruffle 86
Getting ready to sew 18–27
Glossary 126

Hem allowance 42
Hemmed in 40–49
Hems
    blind-stitch hem 44
    corner hem 46–47
    curved hem 45

double hem 43
faced hem 49
narrow hem 43
single hem 42
taped hem 48
Hidden bias binding 77
How a sewing machine works 10
How to run a sewing machine 21

In-seam buttonhole 60
In-seam trim 82
Inset zipper 54
Intersecting seams 39
Inward curve 68
Inward square corner 66

Knife pleats 87

Lapped zipper 56–57

Make me, make me! 96–125
Making bias strip and binding 74–75
Manual buttonhole 59
Mock French seam 35
My sewing machine 8–17

Narrow hem 43

On the edge 72–83
Open seam 34
Outward curve 69
Outward square corner 67

Patchwork 94
Pinning 24
    for basting
    for machine sewing
    pattern pieces
    sewing over pins
Pintucks 89
Piping 81
Pleats
    box pleats 88
    knife pleats 87
Points 70
Pressing 26–27
Projects
    classy cook, the 106–109
    put on the cuffs 122–125
    shop til you drop 110–113
    sleep on it 102–105
    tied up 118–121
    wrapped in ruffles 114–117
    zipped up 98–101
Put on the cuffs 122–125

Quilting 95

Rouleaux loops 62–63

Scallops 70
Seams simple 28–39
Seams
    flat fell seam 38
    French seam 36
    intersecting seams 39
    mock French seam 35
    open seam 34
    self-bound seam 37
    trimming and layering seams 33
Self-bound seam 37
Separating zipper 55
Sewing machine
    buying your first sewing machine 13
    how a sewing machine works 10
    how to run a sewing machine 21
    sewing machine accessories 14
Sewing machine accessories 14
Sewing on lace 91
Sewing on ribbon or braid 90
Sewing on rickrack 90
Sewing straight lines 30
Sewing tools and equipment 16
Shaping bias binding 79
Shop til you drop 110–113
Shortening a zipper 57
Single hem 42
Sleep on it 102–105
Space for sewing, A 20
Starting and finishing sewing 31
Stitches 22
Straight binding

Tailor's ham 27
Taped hem 48
Tension 12
Threads 22
Tied up 118–121
Ties 61
Trimming and layering seams 33

Wrapped in ruffles 114–117

Zigzag bias binding 78
Zipped up 98–101
Zippers
    centered zipper 52–53
    inset zipper 54
    lapped zipper 56–57
    separating zipper 55
    shortening a zipper 57